"Appreciating the Gospels is not easy, especially given all the views that are out there about what the Gospels do with Jesus. Here is a solid introduction to the key themes of these central books about Jesus. Accessible and clear, *Discovering Jesus* will get you well oriented and open up a lifetime of reflection about Jesus."

Darrell L. Bock, Research Professor of New Testament Studies, Dallas Theological Seminary

"Desmond Alexander has produced a concise, readable introduction to the distinctives of each of the four New Testament Gospels and the process of their composition. Written clearly and simply, with helpful charts and diagrams, this small book reflects what a broad cross-section of evangelical New Testament scholars today believe. I recommend it warmly."

Craig L. Blomberg, Distinguished Professor of New Testament, Denver Seminary, and author, co-author, or co-editor of twenty books related to the New Testament

"*Discovering Jesus* has been an invaluable tool for our congregation. We used the charts and outlines for our Gospels class last summer. *Discovering Jesus* helped our people understand each Gospel in a clear and systematic way."

Pablo Monroy, Spiritual Growth and Young Married Pastor, River Pointe Church, Richmond, Texas

D1470250

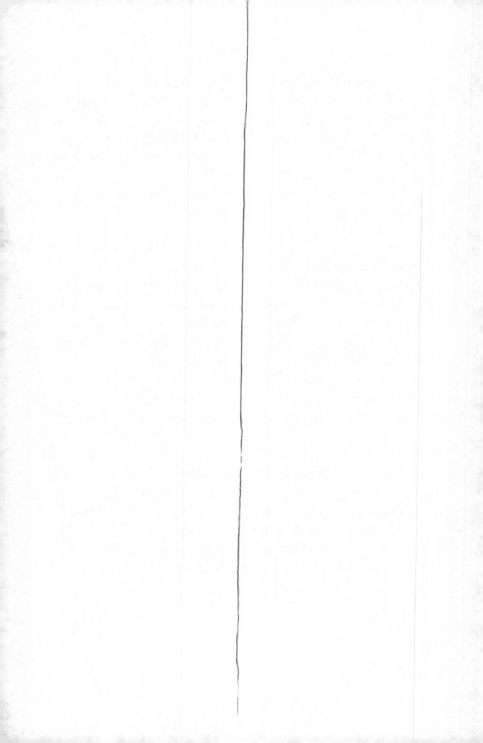

DISCOVERING JESUS

DISCOVERING JESUS

WHY FOUR GOSPELS TO PORTRAY ONE PERSON?

T. D. ALEXANDER

WHEATON, ILLINOIS

Trade paperback ISBN: 978-1-4335-2005-1
PDF ISBN: 978-1-4335-2006-8
Mobipocket ISBN: 978-1-4335-2007-5
ePub ISBN: 978-1-4335-2008-2

Library of Congress Cataloging-in-Publication Data
Alexander, T. Desmond.
    Discovering Jesus : why four Gospels to portray one person /
T. D. Alexander.
        p. cm.
    Includes index.
    ISBN 978-1-4335-2005-1 (tpb) — ISBN 978-1-4335-2006-8 (pdf)
    ISBN 978-1-4335-2007-5 (mobipocket)
    ISBN 978-1-4335-2008-2 (Epub)
    1. Bible. N.T. Gospels—Introductions. I. Title.
BS2555.52.A42   2010
226'.061 — dc22   2010005499

Crossway is a publishing ministry of Good News Publishers.
VP   18   17   16   15   14   13   12   11   10
13   12   11   10   9   8   7   6   5   4   3   2   1

Dedicated to
Renée McCracken
With my thanks

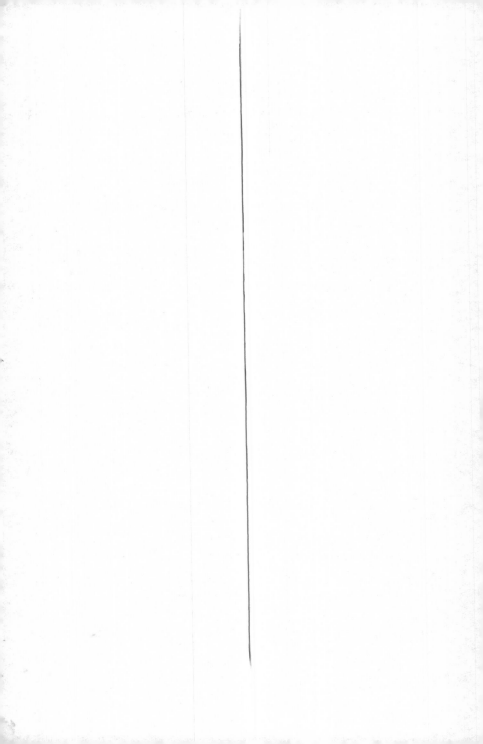

CONTENTS

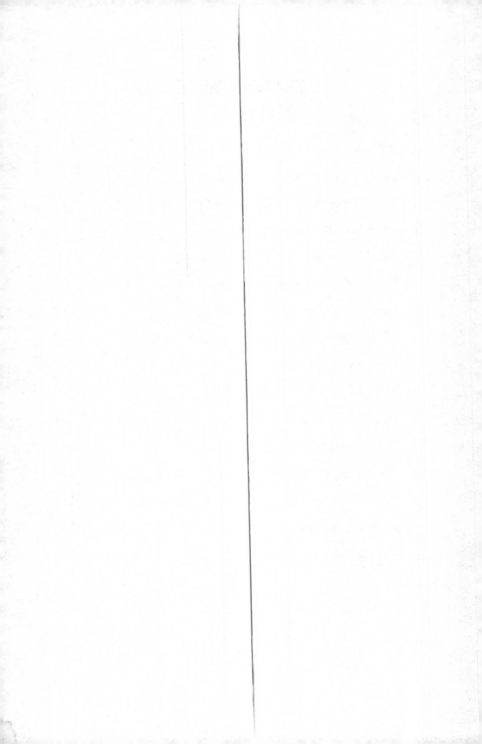

LIST OF CHARTS AND DIAGRAMS

PREFACE

WRITTEN ABOUT two thousand years ago in Greek, the four Gospels are our primary sources of information about the life of Jesus Christ, the most extraordinary person to have ever lived. These authoritative accounts endorsed by the early Christians reveal who Jesus Christ truly is. With good reason, the four Gospels have been highly valued by his followers in every age.

Yet, in spite of this, most Christians do not have a particularly clear understanding of them. Two factors possibly explain this. First, the contents of Matthew, Mark, and Luke overlap considerably. This makes distinguishing between them difficult, and for many Christians, these Gospels tend to blur together. Only John's Gospel stands apart as being noticeably different. Second, the Gospels are often read in piecemeal fashion. Short passages are taken from here and there, without any meaningful attempt being made to see them within the context of a whole Gospel. As a result, exceptionally few Christians, even among those who are educated theologically, are able to describe with certainty the distinctive features and themes of each Gospel.

If you think this is an overstatement, test yourself and your Christian friends with a few questions: How do the Gospels of Mark, Matthew, and Luke differ from each other? What is distinctive about each? How does Mark's picture of Jesus differ from that of Matthew (or Luke, or John)? Why is John's Gospel quite unlike the others? Even mature Christians will struggle to answer these questions.

This very basic lack of knowledge about the Gospels is extremely disturbing, especially given their importance as key witnesses to Jesus Christ. As an attempt to address this problem, this short book provides an opportunity to explore the four Gospels and compare their contents in a largely nontechnical way. The approach adopted is designed to enable ordinary Bible readers to appreciate how the Gospels portray Jesus in four distinctive but complementary ways.

Hopefully, by bringing clarity where there is confusion, this book will help you, the reader, to understand how the four Gospels present Jesus respectively as:

- The son of David who establishes the kingdom of heaven
- The Son of God who suffers to ransom others
- The Savior of the world who seeks the lost
- The Lamb of God who brings eternal life through a new exodus

At a time in history when many well-educated people have only a passing knowledge of what the Bible has to say about Jesus, this introductory guide will enable modern readers to see Jesus through the eyes of his earliest followers. Experiencing Jesus in this way undoubtedly enriches our understanding of who he is, what he has done, and what he continues to do.

The contents of this book first took shape through a course on the Gospels that I taught on several occasions at Union Theological College, Belfast, for church members. The contents have been reworked since then with the hope of making the course materials more widely available, possibly for use in small groups. To prompt discussion and further reflection, questions have been added at the end of each chapter.

It is my hope that this short introduction to the Gospels will prove stimulating, enabling ordinary readers to understand better why the earliest communities of Jesus' followers embraced four accounts of his life. By appreciating the distinctive contribution that each Gospel makes to our understanding of Jesus, we, too, can begin to derive a much richer picture of who he is.

In the process of bringing this book to fruition, I have benefited from the support of many different people. To those who were course participants at the Institute for Christian Training in Union College, I am exceptionally grateful. Their desire to gain a fuller understanding of the Bible has been a particular stimulus to me. For her practical support and encouragement over many years as my secretary, I am deeply indebted to Renée McCracken. It is with pleasure that I dedicate this book to her. Words cannot adequately express my heartfelt thanks to my wife, Anne, and our children, Jane and David, for the wonderful way in which they have enriched my life by surrounding me with a loving family environment. Lastly, but by no means least, I owe my all to the One about whom this book is written; he is indeed everything that the four Gospels proclaim him to be.

SOLI DEO GLORIA

CHAPTER ONE

A BRIEF OVERVIEW
OF THE FOUR GOSPELS

JESUS CHRIST STANDS APART from every other religious leader who has ever lived. Underlining his importance, the Bible contains four remarkable accounts of his life. These four books are known to us by the names of their authors who, according to ancient Christian tradition, are Matthew, Mark, Luke, and John. For centuries these four accounts of the life of Jesus have been called Gospels, the word *gospel* being derived from the Old English term *godspel* meaning "good story." The English word *gospel* translates the Greek word *euangelion*, meaning "good news." This term was used initially to denote the message that Jesus proclaimed. As Mark 1:14 states, ". . . Jesus came into Galilee, proclaiming the gospel [good news] of God." The term, however, soon came to be used of the four accounts of the life of Jesus, probably due to its presence in the opening verse of Mark's Gospel: "The beginning of the gospel [good news] of Jesus Christ, the Son of God."

One thing is immediately striking about the four Gospels. Three of them have a substantial amount of material in common. The Gospels of Matthew, Mark, and Luke frequently share the same contents and, as you shall see, often use exactly the same words. For this reason, most readers find it very difficult to remember in which Gospel a particular incident is narrated. Because they share much in common, the Gospels of Matthew, Mark, and Luke are sometimes referred to as the

Synoptic Gospels; the word *synoptic* comes from the Greek term *sunopsis* meaning "seeing together." John's Gospel stands out as the black sheep of the family, lacking the family characteristics found in Matthew, Mark, and Luke.

In order to give a general picture of how the four Gospels differ from each other, this chapter provides a short overview. In later chapters we shall explore more fully their distinctive themes.

MARK

The shortest of the Gospels is Mark's. Today most scholars believe that it was the first to be composed; the reasons for this are discussed in chapter 11. Mark's compelling record of the life of Jesus exhibits a number of noteworthy features.

MAP 1.1

Mark's Gospel focuses on the adult ministry of Jesus. It tells us nothing about the birth of Jesus, unlike Matthew and Luke. Mark mainly records the actions of Jesus, rather than his teaching. Jesus is portrayed as a very dynamic individual, an image underlined by Mark's style of writing. He often uses the present tense (historical present) to describe past events, giving the impression of of immediacy. This perception is reinforced by his frequent use of the term "immediately" (it appears forty-one times; e.g., Mark 1:10, 12, 18, 20, 21).

The structure of Mark's Gospel follows a clear geographical itinerary which takes the reader from Galilee to Jerusalem. The turning point in the story comes at Caesarea Philippi, north of Galilee, where Peter makes the important affirmation that Jesus is the Christ (Mark 8:27–29). From there the story moves to Jerusalem.

Reflecting the geographical movement of the story, Mark's Gospel displays a relatively straightforward structure, as shown in the chart below.

CHART 1.1

Mark	
1:1–13	Introduction
1:14–6:13	Ministry in Galilee
6:14–8:26	Wider Ministry in the North
8:27–10:52	Toward Jerusalem
11:1–13:37	Confrontation in Jerusalem
14:1–16:8	Passion and Resurrection

This geographical movement from Galilee in the north to Jerusalem in the south is mirrored by a dramatic development in the plot of Mark's Gospel. The story moves from the enthusiasm of the Galilean crowds to the hostility of the Jerusalem authorities. This shift in location plays an important role in explaining why Jesus is eventually put to death. However, as we shall see in chapters 3 and 4, Mark's Gospel has something much more profound to say about the reason behind the crucifixion of Jesus.

MATTHEW

Matthew's Gospel is almost twice the length of Mark's and contains about 90 percent of Mark's material. Not surprisingly, strong similarities exist between the two of them. As the following chart illustrates, Matthew keeps the general geographical-chronological structure used by Mark.

CHART 1.2

	Mark	Matthew
Introduction	1:1–13	1:1–4:11
Ministry in Galilee	1:14–6:13	4:12–13:58
Wider Ministry in the North	6:14–8:26	14:1–16:12
Toward Jerusalem	8:27–10:52	16:13–20:34
Confrontation in Jerusalem	11:1–13:37	21:1–25:46
Passion and Resurrection	14:1–16:8	26:1–28:20

While Matthew has much in common with Mark, there are two important structural differences. First, Matthew adds new material to the beginning and the end of Mark's account.

CHART 1.3

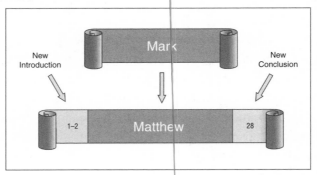

At the start of his Gospel, Matthew introduces additional information concerning the birth of Jesus. In chapter 1, he reveals how Joseph adopts Jesus as his own son, making him heir to the royal line of David. Subsequently, Matthew records the hypocritical reaction of King Herod to the news that learned strangers from the East have come to honor the birth of a new king. By adding this new material to Mark's account, Matthew emphasizes Jesus' royal status. At the end of his Gospel, Matthew includes new information about events that occur after the resurrection of Jesus, emphasizing in particular his return to Galilee. This frames Matthew's account of the adult life of Jesus by bringing the story back to Galilee.

Second, Matthew adds into Mark's mainly action-packed story five blocks of teaching by Jesus.

CHART 1.4

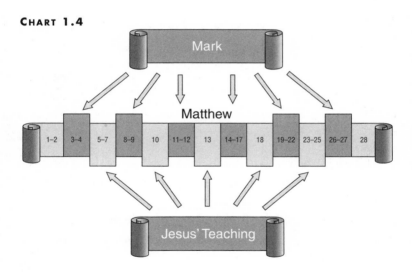

Although Matthew takes over almost all of Mark's material, he is not constrained by Mark's order. Matthew adopts a more topical arrangement and sometimes significantly changes the order in which Mark describes things. While he reorders many of the episodes in Mark's account, Matthew ensures that the five additional blocks of teaching by Jesus are carefully integrated into the whole account. Consequently, the content

of these five speeches harmonizes well with the overall development of Matthew's story.

We shall say more about these features when we look at
Matthew's Gospel in chapters 5 and 6.

LUKE

Luke's Gospel is the first of two volumes, the sequel being the
book of Acts, an account of how the early church expanded,
eventually reaching Rome. Luke's account of the life of Jesus
falls into a number of distinct sections.

CHART 1.5

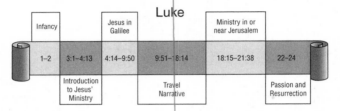

Like Matthew, Luke follows Mark by having the same basic
geographical structure for his account of Jesus' adult life. After
a period of ministry in Galilee, Jesus travels to Jerusalem where
he is crucified. Although Luke borrows much material from
Mark, no Markan material is used in the "Travel Narrative" in
Luke 9:51–18:14.

CHART 1.6

Mark	Luke
1:3–3:19	3:1–6:19
4:1–9:40	8:4–9:50
—	9:51–18:14
10:13–16:6	18:15–24:11

Luke incorporates about half of Mark's Gospel into his biography of Jesus. Like Matthew, he adds new material relating to the birth and resurrection of Jesus.

CHART 1.7

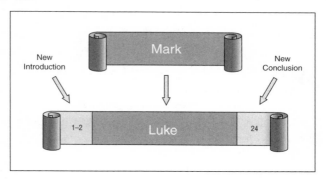

Luke's additions at the start of his Gospel, however, are quite different from those of Matthew. Matthew's introductory chapters focus on the theme of kingship and do so by linking Jesus to the royal line of David. Luke, in marked contrast, records quite different events.

First, Luke has a special interest in the Jerusalem temple. He begins with Zechariah's encountering an angel in the temple. Luke later mentions how Mary and Joseph bring Jesus to the temple to consecrate him to the Lord. Then, as a youth, Jesus views the temple as his "Father's house." Having highlighted the temple in his early chapters, Luke concludes his Gospel with the observation that the disciples "were continually in the temple blessing God."

Second, in his opening two chapters, Luke gives prominence to certain women and also, to a lesser degree, to some shepherds. Remarkably, from a first-century Jewish perspective, God reveals his purposes to these groups. This reflects Luke's special interest in those who were considered to be of lower status within society.

At the conclusion of his Gospel, Luke places Jesus near Jerusalem, whereas Matthew ends with the resurrected Jesus returning to Galilee. Luke is particularly interested in the ascension of Jesus. Not only does Luke conclude his account by mentioning that Jesus "parted from them and was carried up into heaven" (24:51), but he repeats this at the start of Acts (1:9–11). Significantly, Luke makes the same point earlier in Luke 9 as Jesus begins his journey to Jerusalem:

> When the days drew near for him to be taken up, he set his face to go to Jerusalem. (51)

At the very start of Jesus' journey to Jerusalem, Luke wants to highlight the idea of his being "carried up into heaven."

Whereas Mark's Gospel concentrates on the crucifixion of Jesus, Luke's Gospel and the book of Acts emphasize the resurrection and ascension of Jesus. As Peter expresses it in Acts 2:36, (following a long passage on the topic of the resurrection) "God has made him both Lord and Christ, this Jesus whom you crucified." For Luke, the resurrection and ascension of Jesus confirms his true status as the Savior of the world.

Luke's Gospel contains much material that is not found in the other Gospels. Of the twenty-eight parables that he records, fifteen are unique to him. These include such well-known parables as the good Samaritan (the good man from Samaria) and the prodigal son(s). Although Luke includes a considerable quantity of Jesus' teaching, he does not gather it together in blocks as Matthew does.

We shall explore Luke's Gospel in more detail in chapters 7 and 8.

JOHN

John's Gospel is the most distinctive of the four Gospels and shows none of the obvious similarities that exist between the Gospels of Matthew, Mark, and Luke. John does not adopt the geographical-chronological structure that is so apparent in the Synoptic Gospels. Although John notes Jesus' connection with Galilee, he concentrates on Jesus' time in Jerusalem. Unlike Mark and the other Synoptic Gospels, John records three journeys by Jesus to Jerusalem (2:13; 5:1; 7:10). Jesus' presence in Jerusalem is always linked to a festival (e.g., chapter 5 deals with Passover; chapters 7–8 deal with the Feast of Tabernacles). Furthermore, John differs from the Synoptic Gospels by having fewer parables and no exorcisms. By dropping the geographical-chronological structure of the Synoptic Gospels, John has the freedom to shape his account in a very different way. Consequently, the structure of John's Gospel is unique. This also reflects the fact that much of his content has no parallels in the Synoptic Gospels.

John's Gospel falls into two halves. The first half of the Gospel is dominated by two features. First, John draws attention to seven signs (or miracles). These go from the changing of water into wine through to the resurrection of Lazarus. Second, John records a number of dialogues between Jesus and a handful of individuals (e.g., Nicodemus, the woman of Samaria, the man who was ill for thirty-eight years, the man born blind). None of these conversations appear in the Synoptic Gospels.

CHART 1.8

John

| Introduction 1 | Seven Signs and Discourses 2–11 | Passion Narrative 12–19 | Resurrection 20–21 |

John differs from the Synoptic Gospels by having fewer but longer episodes. Professor Graham Stanton notes that they tend to follow a similar pattern: an incident (often a miracle) leads into a dialogue, which in turn is followed by a long monologue (e.g., Nicodemus [3:1–36], the Samaritan woman [4:1–42], the man lying ill by the pool of Bethesda [5:1–47; some manuscripts read Bethzatha], the feeding of the five thousand [6:1–71], Jesus at the feast of tabernacles [7:1–8:59], and the man born blind [9:1–41]).[1]

The second half of John's Gospel is dominated by the Farewell Discourse of Jesus to his disciples (13–17). John differs in his presentation of the Last Supper and the events following it. He does not describe the agony of Jesus in Gethsemane, but rather focuses on the calm and reassured way in which Jesus greeted his captors (18:4). When Jesus affirms, "I am he" (John 18:5), they draw back and fall to the ground (John 18:6). Throughout John's Passion Narrative, Jesus is in control of events.

We shall look in more detail at John's Gospel in chapters 9 and 10.

CONCLUSION

The Gospels of Matthew, Mark, Luke, and John are highly fascinating documents and the relationship between them is complex. Each author has clearly given careful thought to his composition.

In looking at the Gospels we should not lose sight of their overall intention. As the term *gospel* reminds us, they are good news. This good news centers on Jesus Christ. As we shall explore in more detail in subsequent chapters, the four Gospels give us different, but complementary, perspectives on Jesus. The

---

[1] G. N. Stanton, *The Gospels and Jesus*, 2nd ed. (New York: Oxford University Press, 2002), 100.

end result is a very compelling and rich description of a most extraordinary and unique individual.

DISCUSSION QUESTIONS

1. Why do you think that the early church preserved and valued four accounts of the life of Jesus Christ?

2. Which Gospel do you feel most drawn toward? Why?

3. The Gospels of Matthew, Mark, and Luke have much material in common. What makes John's Gospel so different?

4. The Gospels are "good news." How are they still "good news" today?

CHAPTER TWO

COMMON THEMES IN THE GOSPELS

SINCE THE FOUR GOSPELS are all about the life of Jesus Christ, it is only natural that they should contain much material that is similar. And as we have observed in chapter 1, the contents of the Synoptic Gospels overlap considerably. Before concentrating on the distinctive features of each Gospel, we shall consider briefly the main themes that they have in common. These are:

- Fulfillment of Scripture
- Kingdom of God
- Hostility
- Centrality of the passion
- Salvation and the Gentiles
- Importance of faith

FULFILLMENT OF SCRIPTURE

In differing ways all four Gospels present Jesus as fulfilling expectations that are recorded in the Old Testament. This theme of fulfillment is more apparent in Matthew and Luke, although it is not absent from Mark and John. Consequently, all of the Gospels have frequent quotations from or allusions to the Old Testament.

Of the four Gospels, Matthew's offers the most sustained treatment of the theme of fulfillment. Matthew draws attention to this by means of his famous "fulfillment formula" quotations (1:22–23; 2:15, 17–18, 23; 4:14–16; 8:17; 12:17–19; 13:35; 21:4–5; 27:9–10; compare 13:14–15 and 26:56). Using a set pattern of wording, Matthew introduces a quotation from the Old Testament which he sees as being related to the event he is narrating. (Matthew 2:23 is an exception to this rule; here Matthew alludes to an Old Testament concept without giving an exact quotation.) For Matthew, a wide range of interrelated Old Testament promises and expectations are fulfilled in Jesus Christ.

In a similar way, Luke also draws attention to the theme of fulfillment. Perhaps the most significant passage in this connection is Luke's account of how Jesus reads from the book of Isaiah in the synagogue at Nazareth (4:16–30). This passage stands at the very beginning of Luke's description of the adult ministry of Jesus. After reading from Isaiah 61:1–2, Jesus states, "Today this Scripture has been fulfilled in your hearing" (Luke 4:21).

The theme of fulfillment reappears strongly toward the end of Luke's Gospel when he records an encounter between the risen Lord and two disciples traveling to Emmaus. Luke comments, "And beginning with Moses and all the Prophets, he [Jesus] interpreted to them in all the Scriptures the things concerning himself" (24:27). Some verses after this, describing another meeting between the resurrected Jesus and his disciples, Luke records that Jesus said, "These are my words that I spoke to you while I was still with you, that everything written about me in the Law of Moses and the Prophets and the Psalms must be fulfilled" (24:44). The idea that Jesus fulfills promises and expectations recorded in the Old Testament is undoubtedly something that he himself taught.

We shall return to this theme of fulfillment as we look in more detail at the individual Gospels.

KINGDOM OF GOD

One of the most significant themes in the Synoptic Gospels is the kingdom of God. A brief survey of the expression *kingdom of God* reveals that it appears thirteen times in Mark, thirty-two times in Luke, and four times in Matthew. Matthew, however, prefers the alternative expression *kingdom of heaven*, which he uses thirty-two times. When Matthew takes over the phrase *kingdom of God* from Mark, he regularly substitutes the expression *kingdom of heaven* (compare Mark 1:15 with Matthew 4:17). On the basis of Matthew 19:23–24 it seems apparent that *kingdom of God* and *kingdom of heaven* refer to the same thing:

> And Jesus said to his disciples, "Truly, I say to you, only with difficulty will a rich person enter the kingdom of heaven. Again I tell you, it is easier for a camel to go through the eye of a needle than for a rich person to enter the kingdom of God."

Some scholars believe that Matthew may have deliberately substituted the term *heaven* for *God* in order to avoid causing offense to Jewish readers who might have held reservations about pronouncing the word *God*.

In the Synoptic Gospels, the imminent arrival of the kingdom is announced first by John the Baptist:

> In those days John the Baptist came preaching in the wilderness of Judea, "Repent, for the kingdom of heaven is at hand." (Matt. 3:1–2)

In due course Jesus proclaims the same message:

> From that time Jesus began to preach, saying, "Repent, for the kingdom of heaven is at hand." (Matt. 4:17)

Similar statements are found in Mark 1:15 and Luke 4:43. The advent of the kingdom dominates much of Jesus' teaching in the Synoptic Gospels. Matthew devotes the whole of chapter 13 to various parables that highlight the distinctive nature of the coming kingdom (see ch. 6 for more on this).

For the writers of the Synoptic Gospels, the coming of Jesus is intimately connected to the process by which the kingdom of God will be established. Several points are worth observing. First, the arrival of the kingdom of God is tied to repentance. Both John the Baptist and Jesus emphasize the need for people to turn away from their wrongdoing.

Second, the kingdom of God is linked to the proclamation of Jesus as King. This is perhaps most apparent in Matthew's Gospel. In his opening chapters, Matthew associates Jesus with the royal line of David, drawing attention to the visit of the Magi, who come to honor the one who has been born king of the Jews. The theme of Jesus' kingship, which permeates Matthew's Gospel, is particularly prominent in the Passion Narrative. Jesus' entry into Jerusalem is portrayed in regal terms. Later, at his crucifixion the sign placed high on the cross proclaims, "This is Jesus, the King of the Jews" (Matt. 27:37). While Matthew is especially interested in Jesus' royal status, all of the Gospels concur in announcing the remarkable idea that a carpenter's son is heir to the Davidic throne.

Third, the kingdom of God is not presented as a geographical location. Rather it exists where individuals acknowledge the reign of God, with Jesus being his divinely chosen vicegerent. While many of Jesus' contemporaries hoped that the arrival of the kingdom of God would lead to the establishment of Israel as the greatest power on earth, Jesus' teaching on the kingdom points in a very different direction. As the parables of the mustard seed and yeast reveal, the kingdom will begin as something small and grow gradually, perhaps even unnoticed, until, through time, it achieves its full size (Matt. 13:31–33). As we shall see later, Jesus' understanding of how the reign of God would impact the world differed markedly from the expectations of his religious contemporaries.

The four Gospels see the arrival of the kingdom of God as bringing to fulfillment Old Testament expectations. Yet, although the kingdom has come, its consummation lies in the future. While Jesus comes as king, he has not come at this stage to judge and punish the wicked. With his arrival Jesus offers the opportunity for individuals to repent and embrace him as King, or Lord, and Savior. The idea is then introduced that he will return in the future as Judge, and on that occasion, the righteous and the wicked will be separated from each other. As the parables on the kingdom reveal, especially the one concerning the wheat and the weeds, the wicked and the righteous will continue to coexist on earth for some time to come (see Matt. 13:24–30, 36–43).

Although the Gospels proclaim that the kingdom has come and will continue to grow, the establishment of the kingdom in all its fullness and glory will take place in the future. For this reason, Jesus teaches his disciples to pray, "Your kingdom come" (Matthew 6:10). Undoubtedly, all four Gospels encourage their readers to become members of this kingdom and submit to the authority of its King, Jesus Christ.

HOSTILITY

Underlying the story of Jesus is a fundamental recognition that his coming provokes hostility from others, especially those associated with evil. At the beginning of his Gospel, Mark draws attention to the hostile reaction of the unclean spirit toward Jesus. Elsewhere, Jesus is portrayed as being in conflict with Satan.

Remarkably, the main hostility toward Jesus that is consistently presented throughout the Gospels comes from the Jewish religious leaders. Mark wastes little time in his account of Jesus' life in highlighting the opposition of the religious leaders. As early as 3:6, he comments, "The Pharisees went out and immediately held counsel with the Herodians against him, how to destroy him." Because of opposing Jesus and all that he embodies, the religious leaders are presented as siding with the forces of evil.

CENTRALITY OF THE PASSION

The most noteworthy feature of the four Gospels is the emphasis that they all give to the death of Jesus. Almost half of each Gospel is given over to recording the crucifixion and the events immediately surrounding it. Not surprisingly, it is often said that the Gospels are Passion Narratives with extended introductions. The centrality of the passion should not be overlooked. At the heart of the gospel story is the cross. Jesus came not simply to teach or heal, but to die as a sacrifice (Matt. 20:28; Mark 10:45).

As we shall explore in more detail later, the Synoptic Gospels all associate Jesus' death with Peter's confession of him as the Messiah. In all three Synoptic Gospels, Peter's confession of Jesus as the Christ or Messiah is immediately followed by an announcement concerning his suffering and death (Matt. 16:16–21; Mark 8:29–31; Luke 9:20–22). Significantly, this first announcement is then followed by two more (Mark 9:30–32; 10:32–34; compare Matt. 17:22–23; 20:17–19; Luke 9:43–45; 18:31–34). Consequently, each of the Synoptic Gospels has three announcements relating to the future death of Jesus, all coming long before he arrives in Jerusalem.

This concept of a Messiah who would suffer and die

ran counter to common Jewish expectations in Jesus' day. The Gospel writers, however, see this as a fulfillment of Old Testament prophecies, drawing in particular upon the book of Isaiah. Jesus' kingship embraces the concept of a *suffering servant* (see Isaiah 53).

Although John's Gospel differs significantly from the Synoptic Gospels in its overall presentation of the life of Jesus, John also gives prominence to the passion. He draws attention to the sacrificial nature of Jesus' death right at the beginning of his Gospel when he quotes a comment by John the Baptist about Jesus, "Behold, the Lamb of God, who takes away the sin of the world" (John 1:29). For his part, John highlights parallels between Jesus and the exodus from Egypt. Within this framework, Jesus is identified with the Passover lambs that protected the people from death, enabling them to be delivered from bondage in Egypt. For John, the sacrificial death of Jesus brings about a new exodus.

As we shall see in later chapters, the crucifixion of Jesus is an essential component of all four Gospels. Without the cross there can be no good news.

SALVATION AND THE GENTILES

Although the Gospel writers present Jesus as the one promised in the Jewish Scriptures and describe him as the king of the Jews, they reveal that his life has universal significance. For this reason the Gospels proclaim the good news about Jesus to everyone. Having said this, it needs to be recognized that this universal aspect only comes fully into view after the death and resurrection of Jesus. Prior to this, Jesus' mission was directed primarily toward the Jews. Nevertheless, even in this context we can observe in the Gospels material that points to a future Gentile mission. This is especially so with Matthew's Gospel, which is commonly acknowledged to be the most Jewish of the Gospels. Although he appears to write mainly for a Jewish readership, Matthew introduces the idea of the universal nature of Christ's mission in a variety of ways. In his opening genealogy, Matthew draws attention to a number of women who have Gentile connections (e.g., Tamar; Rahab; Ruth; and Bathsheba, the wife of Uriah the Hittite). In chapter 2, he reminds his readers of how foreign Magi sought out the infant Jesus in order to honor him as a new king. In chapter 8, one of the first miracles recorded by Matthew involves the healing of a centurion's servant. Responding to the foreign soldier's request, Jesus comments, "Truly, I tell you, with no one in Israel have I found such faith" (8:10). Later, in an unusual episode that appears to contradict this universal aspect, Jesus initially turns away a Canaanite woman. Her persistence, however, is rewarded and Jesus comments, "O woman, great is your faith! Be it done for you as you desire" (Matt. 15:28).

Although Matthew consistently emphasizes that Jesus' mission was primarily to the lost sheep of Israel, after his death and resurrection Jesus sends his disciples out to all the nations of the earth. With good reason Matthew's Gospel concludes with these words:

> And Jesus came and said to them, "All authority in heaven and on earth has been given to me. Go therefore and make disciples of all nations, baptizing them in the name of the Father and of the Son and of the Holy Spirit, teaching them to observe all that I have commanded you. And behold, I am with you always, to the end of the age." (28:18–20)

While it lies outside the Gospels, Luke's second volume, the book of Acts, highlights the movement of the good news about Jesus from Jerusalem to Samaria, then to Asia Minor, and finally to Rome, at that time the most important city in the world. Luke's account of the early expansion of the Christian church underlines that both Jews and Gentiles are to be united through a common commitment to Jesus Christ as Lord and Savior.

IMPORTANCE OF FAITH

Another major theme in the four Gospels is the emphasis that is given to the concept of faith. References to *faith* and *believing* occur frequently in the Gospels, both words coming from the same root in the Greek language. The first words of Jesus reported by Mark include a call to believe: "The time is fulfilled, and the kingdom of God is at hand; repent and believe in the gospel" (1:15). Throughout the Gospels, Jesus expects individuals to respond by exercising faith. This applies not only to those who want to be healed but also to those who desire to be his disciples. Jesus consistently emphasizes that faith makes people whole (e.g., Mark 5:34; 10:52; Luke 7:50; 17:19; compare Matt. 9:29; 21:22). This emphasis upon faith or believing is perhaps most easily observed toward the conclusion of John's Gospel. Here John gives his reason for writing about Jesus:

> Now Jesus did many other signs in the presence of the disciples, which are not written in this book; but these are written so that you may believe that Jesus is the Christ, the Son of God, and that by believing you may have life in his name. (20:30–31)

All of the Gospel writers encourage people to respond positively by trusting or believing in the One about whom they wrote.

In the Gospels, faith is not about believing a set of doctrines or rules. It is about trusting a person. Not only do the Gospels make Jesus Christ known, but they also place an important challenge before the reader. Do I accept as true what these books have to say about this extraordinary individual? And if I do, will I orientate the whole of my life around him and his teaching?

DISCUSSION QUESTIONS

1. If someone asked you to list the main themes of the Gospels, what would you include in your list?

2. Why is it significant that Jesus brings to fulfillment Old Testament expectations?

3. The Gospels are Passion Narratives with extended introductions. Why is this significant? What does this say about the importance of Jesus' death?

4. Someone may wear a cross to signal that he or she is a Christian. Why is a cross especially appropriate in the light of the four Gospels?

CHAPTER THREE

MARK'S GOSPEL
AND THE SON OF GOD

THE GOSPEL OF MARK is the shortest of the four Gospels. It is now considered by most scholars to have been the first composed, subsequently influencing the writing of both Matthew and Luke. In the light of this factor, we shall begin our detailed study of the individual Gospels by examining Mark's account of the life of Jesus Christ.

AUTHORSHIP

Within the early Christian church it was widely accepted that the author of the shortest Gospel was an individual called Mark. Papias, a bishop in Asia Minor, stated this about AD 130, repeating the words of a presbyter who claimed that Mark obtained his information from Peter:

> When Peter had preached the word publicly in Rome and announced the gospel by the Spirit, those present, of whom there were many, besought Mark, since for a long time he had followed him and remembered what had been said, to record his words. Mark did this, and communicated the gospel to those who made request of him. When Peter knew of it, he neither actively prevented nor encouraged the undertaking. (*Ecclesiastical History 6.14.6–7*)

Papias's account is preserved in Eusebius's *History of the Church* (*Historia Ecclesiastica*) written in AD 325.

WHO IS THIS MARK?

Almost certainly the Mark associated with the authorship of this Gospel is the individual named in the book of Acts (12:12, 25; 13:5, 13; 15:37) and four New Testament Epistles (Col. 4:10; Philem. 1:24; 2 Tim. 4:11; 1 Pet. 5:13). He was the son of a prominent woman in the early church in Jerusalem who later accompanied Paul and Barnabas on their first missionary journey (Acts 12:12). A cousin of Barnabas, he was involved in a dispute that led Paul to part company from Barnabas (Acts 15:37–40). Later, following a reconciliation, Mark appears to have been with Paul in Rome. Peter, also in Rome, mentions that Mark was with him.

Evidence for or against Mark's being the author is hard to find in the Gospel itself. Might he be the unnamed young man, mentioned briefly in Mark 14:51, who flees away naked when Jesus is arrested?

> And they all left him and fled. And a young man followed him, with nothing but a linen cloth about his body. And they seized him, but he left the linen cloth and ran away naked. (Mark 14:50–52)

Since this incident is found only in Mark's Gospel, some scholars believe that it refers to the author. However, the young man's identity is never revealed.

Three main reasons support the idea that Mark, under the influence of Peter, wrote the Gospel. First, of the four Gospels, Mark is the one which is most critical of the twelve disciples, especially Peter. Peter's denial of Jesus is recorded in considerable detail. Given Peter's high standing in the early church, it is unlikely that anyone would have included such negative material without Peter's endorsement. Second, Peter is prominent in Mark's Gospel, and some episodes seem to imply that Peter is the source of the information (see 11:21; 14:72). Third, Mark's

Gospel follows a pattern found in a speech by Peter recorded in Acts 10:36–41 (see Chart 3.1).

None of these arguments decisively proves that Mark was the author of the Gospel. However, in the absence of substantial evidence to the contrary, there is no reason to reject the early Christian tradition of Markan authorship.

CHART 3.1

Mark	Acts 10:36–41
The beginning of the gospel (1:1)	"Good news"
The coming of the Spirit on Jesus (1:10)	"God anointed Jesus of Nazareth with the Holy Spirit."
The Galilean ministry of Jesus focuses on healing and exorcisms. (1:16–8:26)	"Beginning from Galilee . . . He went around doing good and healing all who were oppressed by the devil."
The ministry in Jerusalem (chs. 11–14)	"And we are witnesses of all that he did . . . in Jerusalem."
The death of Jesus (ch. 15)	"They put him to death by hanging him on a tree."
"He has risen; he is not here." (16:6)	"God raised him on the third day."

DATE OF COMPOSITION

Two factors suggest that Mark composed his Gospel around AD 55. First, early Christian sources indicated that Mark wrote the Gospel in Rome, drawing on the preaching of Peter. Peter is known to have been in Rome in the midfifties AD. Second, it is widely believed that Mark's Gospel must have been composed before Luke's. The closely related books of Luke's Gospel and the Acts of the Apostles may have been written in the early sixties; the reference to Paul in prison at the end of Acts suggests a date of composition about AD 62. While we cannot be absolutely certain, the weight of evidence favors placing the composition of Mark's Gospel in the midfifties AD, about twenty-five years after the crucifixion of Jesus.

FOR WHOM WAS THE GOSPEL WRITTEN?

Mark appears to write for Gentiles who live outside Palestine; he translates Aramaic expressions (Mark 3:17; 5:41; 7:11, 34; 15:22) and explains Jewish customs (see Mark 7:3–4). This supports the traditional view that Mark wrote for Christians and others living in Rome. One piece of evidence in favor of this is the number of Latin terms used in the Gospel. In 12:42 Mark equates the two copper coins of the widow with a Roman coin, a *kodrantes* (*quadrans*); in 15:16 the palace is described as a *praitorion*. If Mark had been writing for readers in the eastern part of the Roman Empire, he would more likely have used Greek terms.

THEMES

In describing the life of Jesus, Mark highlights two major themes. First, he is profoundly interested in conveying to his readers the uniqueness of Jesus. As we shall see, he wants to affirm that Jesus is no ordinary person, but rather the Son of God. Second, given who Jesus is, Mark wants to underline the implications of this for his readers. Especially interested in the topic of discipleship, Mark challenges his readers to become followers of Jesus.

In this chapter we shall consider Mark's treatment of the identity of Jesus. We shall deal with the theme of discipleship in our next chapter.

JESUS' IDENTITY

Mark encourages his readers to reflect carefully on who Jesus is. Various questions in the Gospel highlight this interest in the identity of Jesus:

Who can forgive sins but God alone? (Mark 2:7)

Who then is this, that even the wind and the sea obey him? (Mark 4:41)

Where did this man get these things? What is the wisdom given to him? How are such mighty works done by his hands? Is not this the carpenter, the son of Mary and brother of James and Joses and Judas and Simon? And are not his sisters here with us? (Mark 6:2–3)

Questions relating to the identity of Jesus reach a climax when Jesus asks the disciples:

Who do people say that I am? . . . But who do you say that I am? (Mark 8:27–29)

Later, the question of Jesus' true identity lies at the very heart of his trial before the high priest. The high priest asks him, "Are you the Christ, the Son of the Blessed?" (Mark 14:61). In general terms, Mark's Gospel gives two contrasting images of Jesus by way of explaining his identity. The miracle-working power of Jesus in the first half of the Gospel (Mark 1:16–8:26) is set alongside his suffering and death in the second half (Mark 8:27–16:8). By placing these very contrasting, if not almost contradictory, pictures of Jesus side by side, Mark wants to affirm that *Jesus is the Son of God who suffers to ransom others.*

To some extent, Peter's confession, which forms the turning point in Mark's account, draws these two aspects together:

And he asked them, "But who do you say that I am?" Peter answered him, "You are the Christ." And he strictly charged them to tell no one about him. And he began to teach them that the Son of Man must suffer many things and be rejected by the elders and the chief priests and the scribes and be killed, and after three days rise again. (8:29–31)

Whereas the first half of the Gospel highlights the power of Jesus as the Son of God, the second half reveals how Jesus has come to suffer and die in order to redeem people from the power of Satan and death. Through the giving of his life as a ransom, he brings life to others. To appreciate how Mark brings these ideas together, let us begin by focusing on how Jesus is portrayed as the Son of God.

SON OF GOD

As far as Mark himself is concerned there can be no doubt about the identity of Jesus. The opening words of the Gospel state:

> The beginning of the gospel of Jesus Christ, the Son of God.
> (Mark 1:1)

In his opening sentence, Mark makes two important statements about Jesus. First, he is the Christ. The Greek term *christos* refers to someone who has been anointed, usually with oil. As the "anointed one," Jesus is portrayed as having regal status, for in Jewish tradition the kings of ancient Israel were anointed. Significantly, from the Hebrew term for "anointing," *māšîa.h*, we derive the word *Messiah*. At the start of his Gospel, Mark announces that Jesus is the Christ or Messiah.

Second, Mark states unambiguously that Jesus is the "Son of God." This designation is exceptionally important for Mark, and throughout his Gospel he draws attention to Jesus' filial relationship with God in a variety of ways. He notes in particular that this is how God himself refers to Jesus. At the baptism of Jesus and at the transfiguration, God speaks of Jesus as his Son:

> And a voice came from heaven, "You are my beloved Son; with you I am well pleased." (Mark 1:11)

And a cloud overshadowed them, and a voice came out of the cloud, "This is my beloved Son; listen to him." (Mark 9:7)

Unexpectedly, and surprisingly, in Mark's Gospel the testimony of God is supported by the comments of unclean spirits:

What have you to do with us, Jesus of Nazareth? Have you come to destroy us? I know who you are—the Holy One of God. (1:24)

And crying out with a loud voice, he said, "What have you to do with me, Jesus, Son of the Most High God? I adjure you by God, do not torment me." (5:7)

Underlining his divine nature, Mark records elsewhere how Jesus places himself on a par with God by forgiving sins (Mark 2:5–7) and controlling the forces of nature (Mark 4:35–41; 6:45–52). For Mark, Jesus' divinity is revealed through the supernatural things that he is able to do. Yet, even at the crucifixion, when Jesus appears powerless, Mark records how a Gentile centurion remarks that Jesus is the Son of God:

And when the centurion, who stood facing him, saw that in this way he breathed his last, he said, "Truly this man was the Son of God!" (15:39)

This special emphasis upon Jesus's being the Son of God also accounts for Mark's particular interest in the hostility of demonic powers toward Jesus. Mark highlights how the Son of God comes into direct conflict with Satan and those who are associated with him (Mark pays more attention to this than the other Gospel writers.) At the end of his prologue (1:13), Mark introduces briefly the conflict with Satan. Later, Jesus alludes to the binding of Satan (Mark 3:27), and satanic opposition surfaces again when Jesus associates certain comments by Peter with Satan:

But turning and seeing his disciples, he rebuked Peter and said, "Get behind me, Satan! For you are not setting your mind on the things of God, but on the things of man." (Mark 8:33)

The conflict with Satan also includes the confrontation between Jesus and the Jewish leaders. Remarkably, in Mark 3:22 they accuse Jesus of being possessed by Beelzebul, that is, Satan. However, according to Mark, the actions of the Jewish leaders associate them with Satan. Like Satan, they "test" or "tempt" Jesus:

The Pharisees came and began to argue with him, seeking from him a sign from heaven to test him. And he sighed deeply in his spirit and said, "Why does this generation seek a sign? Truly, I say to you, no sign will be given to this generation." (Mark 8:11–12; cf. 10:2)

The hostility between the Jewish leaders and Jesus is also reflected in various passages that involve the concept of ritual cleanness or purity. In Mark 7 the leaders of the Jews claim to be clean and accuse Jesus' disciples of being unclean:

Now when the Pharisees gathered to him, with some of the scribes who had come from Jerusalem, they saw that some of his disciples ate with hands that were defiled, that is, unwashed. (1–2)

In response, Jesus outlines the true nature of cleanness and uncleanness:

And he called the people to him again and said to them, "Hear me, all of you, and understand: There is nothing outside a person that by going into him can defile him, but the things that come out of a person are what defile him." And when he had entered the house and left the people, his disciples asked him about the parable. And he said to them, "Then are you also without understanding? Do you not see that whatever goes into a person from outside cannot defile him, since it enters not his heart but his stomach, and is expelled?" (Thus he declared all foods clean.) And he said, "What comes out of a person is what defiles him. For from within, out of the heart of man, come evil thoughts, sexual immorality, theft, murder, adultery, coveting, wickedness, deceit, sensuality, envy, slander, pride, foolishness. All these evil things come from within, and they defile a person." (Mark 7:14–23)

Closely tied to his confrontation with the Jewish leaders is Jesus' contact with those who were on the fringes of Jewish life: lepers, tax collectors, and sinners. These people were thought unclean either as a result of sinning, illness, or possession by unclean spirits. Mark 5 describes how Jesus heals a man with unclean spirits, cures a woman with a discharge of blood, and raises Jairus's daughter from the dead. All three events demonstrate Jesus' power to transform people who are unclean. This stands in marked contrast to the expectations of the Jewish leaders. Usually, anyone coming into contact with these forms of uncleanness would become unclean. Jesus, however, as the Son of God, has the power to make clean those who are unclean.

Jesus' compassionate approach to those who were on the margins of Jewish society sets him apart from the religious leaders. They feel threatened by his integrity, and in the end their evil nature is revealed. They not only fail to recognize Jesus as the Son of God, but more tellingly they maliciously plot his death. The striking irony in Mark's account is that Jesus, in spite of being the all-powerful Son of God, permits his opponents to execute him. While at one level the cross appears to signal a victory for the powers of evil, more importantly, it is the means by which evil is defeated.

The importance of Jesus' death on the cross also accounts for another unusual feature within Mark's Gospel. Although Mark is very clear about affirming his understanding of Jesus' identity as the Son of God, throughout his account he reveals that those who encounter Jesus are often defective in their understanding or appreciation of him. Everyone seems slow to grasp who Jesus truly is. Two reasons for this should be noted.

First, Jesus himself avoids using the titles "Christ" and "Son of God." Mark is very consistent in noting that Jesus always refers to himself by the title "Son of Man" (Mark 2:10, 28; 8:31, 38; 9:9, 12, 31; 10:33, 45; 13:26; 14:21, 41, 62). This term is, however, ambiguous; it may mean simply *human being* or it may allude to the exceptional person mentioned in Daniel 7:

> I saw in the night visions, and behold, with the clouds of heaven there came one like a son of man, and he came to the Ancient of Days and was presented before him. And to him was given dominion and glory and a kingdom, that all peoples, nations, and languages should serve him; his dominion is an everlasting dominion, which shall not pass away, and his kingdom one that shall not be destroyed. (13–14)

At his trial, Jesus may have Daniel 7 in view when he replied to the high priest:

> Again the high priest asked him, "Are you the Christ, the Son of the Blessed?" And Jesus said, "I am, and you will see the Son of Man seated at the right hand of Power, and coming with the clouds of heaven." (Mark 14:61–62)

Although on this occasion, the expression "Son of Man" appears to take on a deeper significance, this is not necessarily so in other contexts. Consequently, a certain ambiguity exists around Jesus' use of the expression "Son of Man."

Second, Jesus often insists on secrecy. He silences the demons (e.g., Mark 1:25, 34) and instructs those who are healed to tell no one (e.g., Mark 1:44; 5:43). On other occasions he orders his disciples to keep revelations of his glory to themselves (Mark 8:27–30; 9:2–9). In the light of these observations, scholars sometimes refer to this phenomenon as the *messianic secret*, the secret of Jesus' messiahship.

Why does Mark highlight this theme of secrecy? Why does Jesus avoid openly describing himself as the Son of God? The reason is probably to be found in the fact that Mark views the crucifixion of Jesus as the key event for unlocking the identity of Jesus. Everything else that Jesus did only gave an incomplete picture. Any attempt to understand Jesus apart from the cross is defective. Only at the cross do we fully see Jesus as *the Son of God who suffers to ransom others* (see Mark 10:45).

DISCUSSION QUESTIONS

1. Mark introduces his Gospel by telling us that Jesus is the "Son of God." What evidence does he give to support this claim?

2. Jesus is put to death by the Jewish religious leaders. Why might this appear to contradict Mark's claim that Jesus is the Son of God?

3. Mark presents Jesus as the Son of God who suffers to ransom others. Why is this message still very relevant and important for us today?

4. If Jesus confronted you with the question, "Who do you say that I am?" how would you answer?

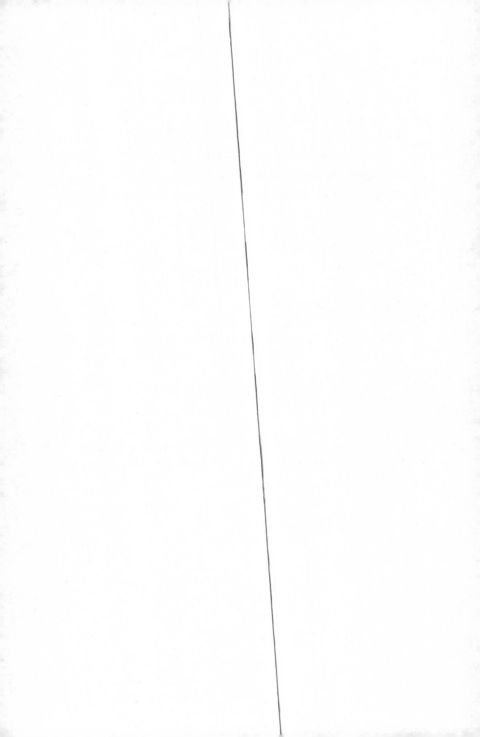

CHAPTER FOUR

MARK'S GOSPEL AND DISCIPLESHIP

IN THE PREVIOUS CHAPTER we saw how Mark presents Jesus as *the Son of God who suffers to ransom others*. To high-light this claim, he initially draws particular attention to the power of Jesus. However, Jesus' status as God's Son brings him into conflict with the forces of evil, especially Satan and those who side with him (e.g., the unclean spirits). Unexpectedly, per-haps, the Jewish religious leaders are also presented as joining with Satan in opposing Jesus. This, in large measure, explains why they are responsible for having Jesus executed on the cross.

Mark, however, indicates that Jesus' death on the cross is not due to his inability to overcome powerful enemies. Rather Jesus gives up his life in order to rescue others from death. The sacrificial nature of Jesus' death is central to understanding who he is and what he achieves. As we shall presently see, the cross is also central to understanding the second major theme of Mark's Gospel–discipleship.

DISCIPLESHIP

Apart from focusing on the theme of Jesus' identity, the Gospel of Mark is a book about following Jesus. The theme of disciple-ship is introduced early in the Gospel when Mark records how Jesus calls some fishermen to follow him:

> Passing alongside the Sea of Galilee, he saw Simon and Andrew the brother of Simon casting a net into the sea, for

they were fishermen. And Jesus said to them, "Follow me, and I will make you become fishers of men." And immediately they left their nets and followed him. And going on a little farther, he saw James the son of Zebedee and John his brother, who were in their boat mending the nets. And immediately he called them, and they left their father Zebedee in the boat with the hired servants and followed him. (1:16–20)

Soon after this Mark describes how Jesus invites Matthew to follow him (2:13–14), and subsequently Jesus appoints the twelve as apostles (3:13–19).

Although Mark notes the initially positive response of those whom Jesus calls, the picture changes as we read on. Mark begins to highlight the blindness of those who follow Jesus, and later he reveals their misconceptions about the nature of true discipleship.

THE BLINDNESS OF THE DISCIPLES

Of all the Gospels, Mark portrays most vividly the shortcomings of the twelve disciples (see 6:52; 8:14–21; 14:32–42). Among their different failings, Mark makes several observations. First, they struggle to understand the meaning of Jesus' parables and require additional explanations:

And he said to them, "To you has been given the secret of the kingdom of God, but for those outside everything is in parables, so that "they may indeed see but not perceive, and may indeed hear but not understand, lest they should turn and be forgiven." And he said to them, "Do you not understand this parable? How then will you understand all the parables?" (Mark 4:11–13)

With many such parables he spoke the word to them, as they were able to hear it. He did not speak to them without a parable, but privately to his own disciples he explained everything. (Mark 4:33–34)

Their hearts are hard. They have little faith and they fail to grasp the significance of Jesus' miracles. To demonstrate this point, Mark records two occasions when Jesus feeds large crowds of people using only a few loaves of bread and some fish. On the first occasion Jesus uses five loaves and two fish to feed five thousand men. Soon afterward, without Jesus, the disciples go by boat across the Sea of Galilee. Mark then records:

> And when evening came, the boat was out on the sea, and he was alone on the land. And he saw that they were making headway painfully, for the wind was against them. And about the fourth watch of the night he came to them, walking on the sea. He meant to pass by them, but when they saw him walking on the sea they thought it was a ghost, and cried out, for they all saw him and were terrified. But immediately he spoke to them and said, "Take heart; it is I. Do not be afraid." And he got into the boat with them, and the wind ceased. And they were utterly astounded, for they did not understand about the loaves, but their hearts were hardened. (6:47–52)

Shortly after this Mark records how Jesus uses seven loaves to feed four thousand men. The disciples and Jesus then undertake another boat journey across the Sea of Galilee. The disciples, however, become confused when Jesus speaks about "the leaven of the Pharisees and the leaven of Herod":

> And Jesus, aware of this, said to them, "Why are you discussing the fact that you have no bread? Do you not yet perceive or understand? Are your hearts hardened? Having eyes do you not see, and having ears do you not hear? And do you not remember? When I broke the five loaves for the five thousand, how many baskets full of broken pieces did you take up?" They said to him, "Twelve." "And the seven for the four thousand, how many baskets full of broken pieces did you take up?" And they said to him, "Seven." And he said to them, "Do you not yet understand?" (Mark 8:17–21)

All of the questions directed to the disciples challenge them regarding their perception of Jesus. Can they not see who he is? Do they not understand?

After this Mark immediately introduces two more incidents that continue the theme of seeing. The first involves the healing of a man who is blind:

> And they came to Bethsaida. And some people brought to him a blind man and begged him to touch him. And he took the blind man by the hand and led him out of the village, and when he had spit on his eyes and laid his hands on him, he asked him, "Do you see anything?" And he looked up and said, "I see men, but they look like trees, walking." Then Jesus laid his hands on his eyes again; and he opened his eyes, his sight was restored, and he saw everything clearly. And he sent him to his home, saying, "Do not even enter the village." (Mark 8:22–26)

Mark notes the gradual process by which this man begins to see. Initially, he sees people, like trees, walking around. Then he sees everything clearly.

Quite deliberately Mark places this unusual healing story immediately prior to Peter's confession of Jesus as the Christ. The restoration of the man's physical sight parallels the way in which Peter and the other disciples gradually come to recognize who Jesus is. They begin to see something of his true identity, but their vision is still blurred. Observe how this is conveyed in Mark 8:27–33:

> And Jesus went on with his disciples to the villages of Caesarea Philippi. And on the way he asked his disciples, "Who do people say that I am?" And they told him, "John the Baptist; and others say, Elijah; and others, one of the prophets." And he asked them, "But who do you say that I am?" Peter answered him, "You are the Christ." And he strictly charged them to tell no one about him.

> And he began to teach them that the Son of Man must
> suffer many things and be rejected by the elders and the chief
> priests and the scribes and be killed, and after three days rise
> again. And he said this plainly. And Peter took him aside and
> began to rebuke him. But turning and seeing his disciples, he
> rebuked Peter and said, "Get behind me, Satan! For you are
> not setting your mind on the things of God, but on the things
> of man."

Although Peter is correct in recognizing that Jesus is the
Christ, his subsequent actions and words reveal that he has
grasped only partially the significance of this. He has yet to
comprehend fully the necessity of Jesus' death on the cross.
As the following chapters in Mark's Gospel make clear, Jesus'
messiahship can only be understood in the light of his sacrificial
death. The cross is central to knowing who Jesus is.

THE CROSS AND DISCIPLESHIP

Not only is the cross key to understanding who Jesus is, but it
is also the pattern for discipleship. In chapters 8–10 of Mark,
Jesus links the description of his own suffering and death with
comments about discipleship. From 8:27 through 10:52, Mark
concentrates on what it is to be a true disciple. To be a follower
of Jesus is to go the Jesus way of humility, rejection, and suffering—the way of the cross.

This point is underlined by Mark when he repeats the same
narrative pattern three times. On three separate occasions Jesus
refers to his suffering, rejection, death, and resurrection: Mark
8:31; 9:31; 10:33–34. Clearly there was no ambiguity about
what Jesus said, for Mark comments in 8:32, "And he said this
plainly." Yet, the reaction of the disciples shows that they mis-
understood Jesus. Jesus then responds by teaching them about
the true nature of discipleship. We can illustrate this pattern
using a simple chart.

CHART 4.1

Place	Prediction	Confusion	Teaching
Caesarea 8:27	8:31	8:32–33	8:34–38
Galilee 9:30	9:31	9:33–34	9:35–37
Judea 10:1	10:33–34	10:35–41	10:42–45

The first reference to the cross as the way of discipleship comes after Peter's confession of Jesus as the Christ at Caesarea Philippi. Jesus has to rebuke Peter because he is not willing to accept that Jesus' messiahship will involve suffering, rejection, and death. Jesus then emphasizes that discipleship involves taking up the cross:

> And calling the crowd to him with his disciples, he said to them, "If anyone would come after me, let him deny himself and take up his cross and follow me. For whoever would save his life will lose it, but whoever loses his life for my sake and the gospel's will save it. For what does it profit a man to gain the whole world and forfeit his soul? For what can a man give in return for his soul? For whoever is ashamed of me and of my words in this adulterous and sinful generation, of him will the Son of Man also be ashamed when he comes in the glory of his Father with the holy angels." (Mark 8:34–38)

The second reference to the death of Jesus (Mark 9:31) is immediately followed by the comment, "But they did not understand the saying, and were afraid to ask him" (Mark 9:32). Mark then records how the disciples inappropriately discuss among themselves, "Who is the greatest?" In response Jesus teaches them again about the nature of true discipleship: "If anyone would be first, he must be last of all and servant of all" (Mark 9:35).

A similar pattern is repeated with the third passion prediction. After Jesus refers to his betrayal and death (Mark

10:33–34), James and John ask that they may sit on either side of Jesus in his glory (Mark 10:35–37). Jesus, however, replies with these words:

> You know that those who are considered rulers of the Gentiles lord it over them, and their great ones exercise authority over them. But it shall not be so among you. But whoever would be great among you must be your servant, and whoever would be first among you must be slave of all. For even the Son of Man came not to be served but to serve, and to give his life as a ransom for many. (Mark 10:42–45)

The threefold repetition of Jesus' teaching on discipleship that comes in chapters 8, 9, and 10 underlines the importance of this theme in Mark's story. The disciples looked for triumph and glory. Jesus anticipated self-denial and suffering. The climax comes in Mark 10:45: "For even the Son of Man came not to be served but to serve, and to give his life as a ransom for many." All importantly, Mark highlights that the death of Jesus is *a ransom for many*.

The Jewish contemporaries of Jesus expected a triumphant, powerful, kinglike Messiah who would usher in a new age of prosperity and peace, accompanied by the defeat of their enemies. In the light of this, Jesus' disciples probably looked forward to a triumphant life as his followers. Jesus, however, has a very different understanding of the role of the Messiah—martyrdom rather than triumphalism. Jesus' disciples had to learn that messiahship and discipleship involved suffering, even death. The disciples of Jesus must resemble him; like Jesus, his disciples must walk the path of humility, suffering, and even death (see Mark 8:34).

By associating discipleship with the cross, Mark emphatically binds these two concepts together. To become a follower of Jesus is to go the way of the cross. While Mark refuses to diminish the cost of following Jesus, he motivates his readers by presenting the first disciples as examples from whom others may learn. We can take comfort from the fact that in spite of their many failings, Jesus did not reject those who decided to follow him.

DISCUSSION QUESTIONS

1. Mark wants to persuade his readers that they, too, should follow Jesus. How does he weave this theme into his Gospel?

2. In Mark 8:34–38 Jesus describes discipleship using the image of a cross. Why does Jesus link together the cross and discipleship?

3. Jesus' own experience is meant to be a model for his disciples. In the light of Mark 10:42–45, what can we learn from Jesus about serving others?

4. Mark frames his threefold presentation of the teaching of Jesus on discipleship in 8:31–10:45 with two episodes about blind men being healed (Mark 8:22–26 and 10:46–52). What differences are there in the two healing processes? Why might it be significant that Mark has included these incidents before and after Jesus' teaching on the cross and discipleship?

CHAPTER FIVE

MATTHEW'S GOSPEL
AND CONFLICT

THE GOSPEL OF MATTHEW appears to have been the most widely used in the early church. Its popularity is reflected in the fact that for the first three centuries after the birth of Christ, it is the most frequently quoted Gospel. The earliest surviving documents that refer to Matthew are the epistles of Ignatius (ca. AD 110–115).

WHO WROTE MATTHEW'S GOSPEL?

The author has traditionally been taken to be Matthew (or Levi), whose call to follow Jesus is recorded in Matthew 9:9:

> As Jesus passed on from there, he saw a man called Matthew sitting at the tax booth, and he said to him, "Follow me." And he rose and followed him.

Scholars have debated at length whether Matthew could have written the Gospel. The available evidence is very limited, and the Gospel itself offers few clues about the identity of its author. Consider, however, two observations that support the traditional view of Matthean authorship. First, Matthew was able to write fluent Greek. As a tax collector answering to the Romans, Matthew would have needed to be competent in the Greek language. He would also have been literate in order to keep records. Second, since Matthew does not stand out in a special way among the disciples of Jesus, why would he have been credited as the author by the early church if there was no basis for this in real life?

FOR WHOM WAS THE GOSPEL WRITTEN?

Alongside the book of Hebrews, the Gospel of Matthew is one of the most Jewish books in the New Testament. Matthew appears to have been written by a Jewish follower of Jesus for a Jewish-Christian audience. There is a distinctly "Semitic" touch to some of Matthew's Greek. Some Aramaic terms remain untranslated (e.g., *raka* "fool," 5:22; *korbanas* "treasury," 27:6), and some customs are unexplained (e.g., hand-washing, 15:2, compare Mark 7:3–4; the wearing of phylacteries, 23:5). The author of the Gospel assumes that his readers will understand these things.

Much of the content of Matthew's account appears to have been selected to appeal to Jewish readers. The Gospel begins with a genealogy descending from Abraham to Jesus, and records frequent references to Jesus as the "son of David." Of the four Gospels, Matthew quotes or alludes to the Old Testament most often. Matthew also uses the more Jewish expression *kingdom of heaven* rather than *kingdom of God*. Many of the specific issues mentioned in Jesus' teaching would be of special interest to Jewish readers (e.g., fasting, the Sabbath, temple offerings, the temple tax). All of these factors strongly suggest that Matthew's Gospel was penned for readers from a Jewish background.

DATE OF COMPOSITION

On the assumption that Matthew knew the Gospel of Mark, his account could not have been written earlier than AD 55. Some scholars suggest a date after AD 70 on the basis that Matthew's

Gospel possibly displays a knowledge of the destruction of Jerusalem in AD 70. This, however, is open to debate.

RELATIONSHIP TO MARK

Most biblical scholars believe that Matthew's longer account of the life of Jesus is based upon the Gospel of Mark. Comparing the two books, roughly 45 percent of Matthew's Gospel consists of material found in Mark. Of the 661 verses in Mark, more than 600 appear in Matthew; of these about half are identical as regards the actual wording. Much of the additional material in Matthew consists of discourses or speeches by Jesus.

As we have already noted in chapter 1, Matthew expands upon Mark's account by adding material at the beginning and the end.

CHART 5.1

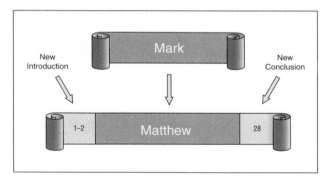

Matthew also incorporates into the mainly action-packed story of Mark, five blocks of teaching by Jesus (see Chart 5.2). Each of the five sections of Jesus' teaching added by Matthew concludes with a similar statement—"And when Jesus had finished saying these things . . . " (Matt. 7:28; cf. 11:1; 13:53; 19:1; 26:1).

CHART 5.2

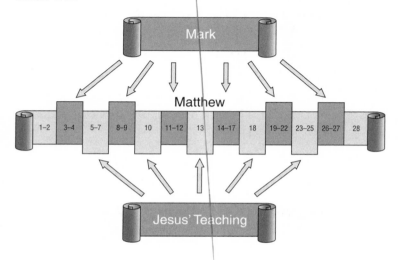

As well as inserting the five speeches, Matthew reorganizes the order in which Mark tells the story. Matthew adopts a much more topical approach; the material is organized by subject matter and not simply chronology. We can see this very clearly in Matthew 5–9. See first how Matthew refers in a summary statement to the teaching, preaching, and healing ministry of Jesus:

> And he went throughout all Galilee, teaching in their synagogues and proclaiming the gospel of the kingdom and healing every disease and every affliction among the people. (4:23)

Matthew then proceeds to illustrate this. After focusing on Jesus' teaching in chapters 5–7 (the Sermon on the Mount), Matthew concentrates chiefly on Jesus' miraculous healing activity in chapters 8–9. Placing this material after the Sermon on the Mount, Matthew demonstrates that Jesus fulfills the two major aspects of this mission—teaching and healing. The words and actions of Jesus are linked by the following verses:

And when Jesus finished these sayings, the crowds were astonished at his teaching, for he was teaching them as one who had authority, and not as their scribes. (Matt. 7:28–29)

Whereas Matthew draws attention in the Sermon on the Mount to the authority of Jesus' teaching, in chapters 8–9 he focuses on Jesus' authority as revealed in his actions.

By comparing Matthew's account with that of Mark and Luke, it is apparent that Matthew arranges the material in chapters 8–9 on topical, not chronological grounds. All of the incidents recorded in these two chapters are found either in Mark (mainly 1:40–2:22) or Luke. Chronologically speaking, the events recorded in Matthew 8:2–4, 14–17; 9:2–13 probably all took place before Jesus taught the Sermon on the Mount (see Mark 1:29–34, 40–45; Luke 4:38–41). In contrast, the incident found in Matthew 8:18–22 probably happened much later and, strictly speaking, should come after Matthew 13 (see Luke 8:22–56). Matthew deliberately ignores the chronological order of events in order to arrange his material in a way that highlights particular themes. His record of each incident also tends to be the shortest of all the Gospel writers'.

Although Matthew reorganizes much of the material that he borrows from Mark, it is hardly surprising that he repeats some of the important themes found in Mark. About 90 percent of Mark is found in Matthew. Not surprisingly, therefore, the theme of conflict, which is significant in Mark, is developed further by Matthew.

THE THEME OF CONFLICT

According to J. D. Kingsbury, the plot of Matthew's Gospel is about conflict. Reflecting this, the opening chapters of Matthew introduce Jesus as the main character and the religious leaders as his antagonists. Kingsbury summarizes the portrayal of Jesus and his opponents as follows. Jesus is the "Messiah, the Anointed One, Israel's long-awaited King." He is also the Son of God, enjoying a "unique filial relationship with God," being "wholly obedient" to his Father, and acting on his Father's behalf as the one through whom God will bring salvation to humanity.[1]

In marked contrast, the religious leaders are initially portrayed as assisting King Herod in finding the young Messiah (Matt. 2:1–6). Soon afterwards the Pharisees and Sadducees make a more prominent appearance in Matthew 3:7–10, where John the Baptist refers to them as a "brood of vipers" (Matt. 3:7). By contrasting Jesus and the religious leaders, the opening chapters of Matthew clearly foreshadow how the story will develop.

After introducing the antagonists, Matthew presents in chapters 5–9 a largely positive picture of Jesus. Many people respond favorably to his teaching and healing. However, some criticism of Jesus is implied by the comments of the Pharisees in Matthew 9:4 and 9:11. On the first occasion, they keep their criticism to themselves. On the second, they express it to Jesus' disciples, but not to Jesus himself. These preliminary criticisms prepare the way for a more sustained attack on Jesus in chapter 12. Interestingly, Matthew presents Jesus as anticipating this in his speech in chapter 10.

The final main section of Matthew's story (16:21–28:20) begins with a reference to Jesus' journey to Jerusalem, predicting his suffering, death, and resurrection (16:21). There are then two more passion predictions in 17:22–23 and 20:17–19. On account of these predictions, the reader expects the conflict to intensify when Jesus reaches Jerusalem. Finally, in the wake of Jesus' triumphal entry into Jerusalem (Matt. 21:1–11), the conflict comes to a climax (Matt. 21:12–22:46)

Kingsbury highlights five literary devices in Matthew 21–22

---

[1] J. D. Kingsbury, "The Plot of Matthew's Story," *Interpretation* 46, (1992): 347–56.

that show the magnitude of the conflict between the religious leaders and Jesus.

1. The setting is the temple, the seat of authority for the religious leaders and the place of God's presence.
2. On each occasion the Jewish leaders confront Jesus directly. They wish to get the better of him (Matt. 21:15, 23; 22:16–17, 23–28, 35–36). However, this pattern is eventually broken when in the final controversy "Jesus seizes the initiative and puts the Pharisees on the spot" (Matt. 22:41–46).
3. The issue in each controversy centers on the topic of authority. This arises after Jesus cleanses the temple (Matt. 21:23–27) and reappears when questions are asked about the interpretation of Scripture and the law (Matt. 22:17, 24, 36, 43–45).
4. Matthew parades a long list of Jesus' opponents—"the chief priests, the scribes, the elders of the people, the disciples of the Pharisees, the Herodians, the Sadducees, a Pharisaic lawyer, and the Pharisees (21:15, 23; 22:16, 23, 34–35, 41)." This underlines the intensity of the conflict during a period of several days and reveals that those who oppose Jesus represent a wide diversity of viewpoints.
5. Matthew characterizes "the atmosphere in which this conflict takes places as being extremely hostile." He even mentions that the Pharisees want to arrest Jesus but hold back for fear of the crowds:

When the chief priests and the Pharisees heard his parables, they perceived that he was speaking about them. And although they were seeking to arrest him, they feared the crowds, because they held him to be a prophet. (Matthew 21:45–46)[2]

---

[2]Ibid., 353–54.

Eventually, even fear of the crowd is overcome and the leaders of the Pharisees succeed in having Jesus executed. Normally, this would be the end of the story. However, the resurrection of Jesus turns everything on its head. The apparent victory of his opponents has been merely temporary, and with his resurrection, Jesus' status as Messiah and Son of God is confirmed.

ANTI-JEWISH?

The theme of conflict produces a remarkable contrast in Matthew's Gospel. In spite of being the most Jewish of the Gospels, Matthew's account is also the most *anti-Jewish* or to be much more accurate *anti-some-Jewish-religious-leaders*. This distinction is important to note, as unfortunately it has not always been appreciated, resulting tragically in unwarranted anti-Semitic hostility.

Writing to Jews, Matthew needs to explain why Jesus was put to death at the insistence of the Jewish authorities. How could this possibly happen to the divinely appointed King of the Jews? This issue best explains the harsh criticism that Matthew's Gospel records concerning the Pharisees and teachers of the law. We see this especially in chapter 23. Here, among many other things, Jesus passionately states:

> Woe to you, scribes and Pharisees, hypocrites! For you are like whitewashed tombs, which outwardly appear beautiful, but within are full of dead people's bones and all uncleanness. So you also outwardly appear righteous to others, but within you are full of hypocrisy and lawlessness. (Matt. 23:27–28)

Hypocrisy underlies much of what the religious leaders do. A vivid example of this comes in Matthew 12 when Jesus heals a man on the Sabbath:

> He went on from there and entered their synagogue. And a man was there with a withered hand. And they asked him, "Is it law-

ful to heal on the Sabbath?"—so that they might accuse him. He said to them, "Which one of you who has a sheep, if it falls into a pit on the Sabbath, will not take hold of it and lift it out? Of how much more value is a man than a sheep! So it is lawful to do good on the Sabbath." Then he said to the man, "Stretch out your hand." And the man stretched it out, and it was restored, healthy like the other. But the Pharisees went out and conspired against him, how to destroy him. (9–14)

Tellingly Matthew records, "Looking for a reason to accuse Jesus, they asked him, 'Is it lawful to heal on the Sabbath?'" Whereas Jesus uses the Sabbath to bring healing, the Pharisees use it as an occasion to bring death. As Matthew observes, they "went out and conspired against him, how to destroy him" (Matt. 12:14). Presumably, they did so on the Sabbath.

The hostility of the Jewish religious leaders centers on Jesus' claim to have authority from God. Everything that Jesus does is perceived by the religious leaders as a threat to their position within Jewish society. Sadly, the leaders of the people have lost their way, and their actions reveal that they have more in common with Satan than with God. As a Jewish follower of Jesus, writing primarily to Jews, Matthew wants to affirm that Jesus is the one sent by God to establish his authority over the earth.

For Matthew, Jesus' authority surpasses that of the religious leaders because he is the true heir to the Davidic throne. As we shall unpack further in our next chapter, Matthew is especially interested in portraying Jesus as *the son of David who establishes the kingdom of heaven.*

DISCUSSION QUESTIONS

1. Matthew arranges much of his Gospel topically. In chapters 8–9 he concentrates largely on the healing activities of Jesus. How does Matthew's choice of materials convey the extent of Jesus' power and authority?

2. The triumphal entry of Jesus into Jerusalem in Matthew 21:1–11 provokes the Jewish religious leaders to intensify their hostility toward Jesus. Why do the manner of Jesus' arrival and his subsequent actions anger the religious leaders so much?

3. Although the Jewish religious leaders fail to grasp the true identity of Jesus, others of lesser standing are more perceptive. What lesson might we draw from this about how people respond to Jesus today?

4. Regrettably, some Christians have mistakenly adopted anti-Jewish attitudes. How might Matthew's Gospel be misinterpreted to support such an outlook?

CHAPTER SIX

MATTHEW'S GOSPEL AND THE SON OF DAVID

AT THE VERY HEART OF Matthew's Gospel is the idea that Jesus is king. In a rich variety of ways, Matthew underlines Jesus' royal status by presenting him as heir to the Davidic dynasty. To understand all that this entails, we shall explore in this chapter a number of interrelated issues:

- Jesus Christ, the son of David
- The kingdom of heaven
- The fulfillment of Old Testament expectations
- The kingdom of heaven and Jews
- The kingdom of heaven and Gentiles

JESUS CHRIST, THE SON OF DAVID

Matthew's Gospel begins, like Mark's, with a clear statement about the identity of Jesus Christ. However, whereas Mark announces that Jesus is the *Son of God*, Matthew affirms that Jesus is the *son of David*:

> The book of the genealogy of Jesus Christ, the son of David, the son of Abraham. (1:1)

For Matthew, the designation *son of David* is clearly very important. Indeed, it appears more often in Matthew than in all of the other books of the New Testament combined. By describing Jesus as the son of David, Matthew points to Jesus' royal status as heir to the dynasty descended from David, the first Israelite king of Jerusalem. Remarkably, the title *son of David* is never used by Jesus of himself, apart from 22:41–45 when he challenges the Pharisees regarding their understanding of the term. Yet even in this context, Jesus does not directly claim to be the son of David.

The designation *son of David* is used most frequently in contexts that focus on the healing power of Jesus (Matt. 9:27; 15:22; 20:30–31; compare 12:22–23; 21:14–15). Other people call Jesus the son of David. Why Jesus' healing power should be linked to the title *son of David* is not clear. Perhaps it focuses attention away from the national, political restoration that many Jews associated with the Messiah or son of David. Another possible, and even complementary, explanation is based on the observation that those who use this title are people of no social or theological importance—the blind, the lame, the dumb, a Canaanite woman with a demon-possessed daughter. Ironically, it is the physically blind and the Gentiles who identify Jesus' true status, whereas the Jewish religious leaders do not.

Apart from frequently using the title *son of David*, Matthew highlights the son of David theme by introducing a genealogy at the start of the Gospel. This genealogy links Jesus to David, although in a rather surprising way. David's descendant Joseph is not presented as the biological father of Jesus. Matthew makes it clear that this is not the case. Rather, Matthew reveals that Joseph adopts Jesus as his legitimate heir. By way of supporting his claim that Jesus is the son of David, Matthew employs a number of other titles for Jesus, all of which have royal connotations. These include *Christ, Lord,* and *Son of God.*

Christ

As well as introducing Jesus as the son of David, Matthew 1:1 also uses the term *Christ.* In our contemporary usage the words

Jesus Christ are taken to be a name. However, in Matthew 1:1 and 1:18 *Christ* is used as a title, meaning "the anointed one." This underlines Jesus' royal status, reflecting the tradition of Israelite kings being anointed in the Old Testament.

Having noted the presence of the title *Christ* in 1:1, it occurs only rarely in the rest of the Gospel with reference to Jesus. In 11:2 it is introduced by the narrator in the context of John the Baptist's disciples' inquiring regarding Jesus' identity; here it clarifies their question regarding "the one who is to come" (Matt. 11:3). In Matthew 16:16, 20, Peter confesses Jesus to be the Christ. Jesus himself uses the term regarding false messiahs (Matt. 24:5, 23; see also 23:10). Later, the High Priest seeks to know if Jesus is the Christ (Matt. 26:63). In its final three occurrences the title *Christ* is used as a taunt or accusation (Matt. 26:68; 27:17, 22).

At no point does Matthew indicate that Jesus used the title *Christ* of himself, although Matthew clearly believes that it is an appropriate title for him. The reluctance of Jesus to use this title is probably due to the connotations that it had at that time in Judea. For Jesus, the popular definition or understanding of *Christ* was inadequate and erroneous, for it had largely political connotations. This did not reflect accurately how the Old Testament portrayed the future, divinely promised king of the Davidic line.

Lord

In Matthew, the disciples consistently refer to Jesus as *Lord* (Gk., *kurie*). They use the term *Lord* twenty-five times, but never *teacher*. The opponents of Jesus use the term *Teacher* (Gk., *didaskale*, which translates the Aramaic *rabbi* or *rabbouni*; compare Matt. 26:25 [also v. 49] with 26:22; whereas each of the disciples asks, "Is it I, Lord?" Judas remarks, "Is it I, Rabbi?").

Given Matthew's use of *kurios*, "lord," it has to be asked if this is understood by Matthew to be a divine name of majesty. In the Greek translation of the Old Testament (LXX) *ho kurios*, "the Lord," is used as the name for God. From within Matthew's Gospel it is clear that the word *kurios* is occasionally used as a term of respect without any suggestion of deity (e.g., Matthew 13:27; 21:30; 25:20, 22, 24; 27:63). Nevertheless, on occasions Matthew does perhaps associate the term *kurios* with the concept of divine authority (e.g., Matt. 7:21, 22; 25:37, 44).

Son of God
Like Mark, Matthew gives prominence to the idea that Jesus is the Son of God. Each time God speaks about Jesus he declares him to be his Son (e.g., Matt. 3:17; 17:5). Immediately after the first of these occasions the Devil questions this title—"If you are the Son of God . . . " (Matt. 4:3, 6).

Alongside references to Jesus as the Son of God, Jesus refers to God as Father forty-four times in Matthew; Mark has four such references, and Luke, seventeen. Of the forty-four references to God as Father in Matthew, half involve Jesus' relationship with God; the rest involve the disciples. However, a distinction is drawn between "your Father" and "my Father," indicating that Jesus enjoys a unique filial relationship with God.

In the Old Testament, the Davidic King is sometimes described as God's son (2 Sam. 7:14; Ps. 2:7; 89:26–27). In the light of this, the title *Son of God* can be viewed as supporting Matthew's claim that Jesus is heir to the Davidic throne. In fact, all of the terms used of Jesus—*son of David, Christ, Lord, Son of God*—should be understood as pointing to his royal nature. This theme of royalty extends across Matthew's Gospel from the visit of the Magi to the execution of Jesus on the cross.

From all that Matthew says, it is clear that Jesus is no ordinary son of David. One passage, in particular, highlights this issue, coming at a particularly significant point in Matthew's account. At the end of chapter 22, following a series of episodes in which Jesus' opponents question him, Jesus then challenges the Pharisees regarding their understanding of the expression *son of David*:

> Now while the Pharisees were gathered together, Jesus asked them a question, saying, "What do you think about the Christ? Whose son is he?" They said to him, "The son of David." He said to them, "How is it then that David, in the Spirit, calls him Lord, saying, 'The Lord said to my Lord, Sit at my right hand, until I put your enemies under your feet'? If then David calls him Lord, how is he his son?" And no one was able to answer him a word, nor from that day did anyone dare to ask him any more questions. (Matt. 22:41–46)

Without going into this passage in detail, Jesus interprets Psalm 110 as implying that the son of David will be greater than David himself. In saying this, Jesus rebukes the Pharisees for having an inadequate understanding of what the promised son of David will do.

THE KINGDOM OF HEAVEN

Closely associated with Jesus' status as king is the concept of the kingdom of heaven or the kingdom of God. John the Baptist and Jesus both proclaim the coming of the kingdom, urging their listeners to prepare for it. While everything that Jesus teaches relates in some way to this kingdom, Matthew 13 records seven parables that provide important insights into the nature of the kingdom of heaven:

- First, the kingdom will grow gradually, starting as something small but eventually reaching full maturity.

- Second, during this growing phase, the Devil will actively seek to hinder the kingdom's growth.
- Third, at the end of this growing phase, a time of judgment will come when the righteous and the wicked will be separated. This will have disastrous consequences for the wicked.
- Fourth, individuals are challenged to submit to the authority of Jesus as King. Nothing is more important. To be within the kingdom is worth everything that a person possesses. Unfortunately, not all who initially respond positively will remain submissive to Jesus' authority.

THE FULFILLMENT OF OLD TESTAMENT EXPECTATIONS

One of the distinctive features of Matthew's Gospel is the use of formula quotations—"to fulfill (or "then was fulfilled") what had been spoken by the prophet, saying. . . ." Slight variations in the formula exist, Matthew 2:23 being the most noteworthy. Here the mention of "prophets" and the omission of "saying" suggest that this is not an exact quotation but rather a reference to a general prophetic theme:

> And he went and lived in a city called Nazareth, that what was spoken by the prophets might be fulfilled: "He shall be called a Nazarene." (Matt. 2:23)

Including Matthew 2:23, there are ten passages that use the fulfillment formula (Matt. 1:22–23; 2:15, 17–18, 23; 4:14–16; 8:17; 12:17–21; 13:35; 21:4–5; 27:9–10). Possibly 2:5–6 could also be included, but the verb *pleroo*, "to fulfill," is not used on this occasion, and the quotation from Micah 5:2 is written in the context of the chief priests and teachers of the law informing Herod regarding the birthplace of the Messiah.

Matthew's use of Old Testament quotations has been discussed by scholars at some length, and it is not possible to cover everything here. It should be noted, however, that Matthew uses them in a creative way. Usually we are meant to focus not merely on the words quoted, but on the larger context from which they are drawn. Furthermore, the fulfillment of the Old Testament quotation is not always confined to its immediate context in the story. Take, for example, Matthew 4:15–16 which quotes from Isaiah 9:1–2:

> And leaving Nazareth he went and lived in Capernaum by the sea, in the territory of Zebulun and Naphtali, so that what was spoken by the prophet Isaiah might be fulfilled: "The land of Zebulun and the land of Naphtali, the way of the sea, beyond the Jordan, Galilee of the Gentiles—the people dwelling in darkness have seen a great light, and for those dwelling in the region and shadow of death, on them a light has dawned." (Matt. 4:13–16)

The context of this quotation from Isaiah 9 concerns the promise of a future, outstanding Davidic king:

> For to us a child is born, to us a son is given; and the government shall be upon his shoulder, and his name shall be called Wonderful Counselor, Mighty God, Everlasting Father, Prince of Peace. Of the increase of his government and of peace there will be no end, on the throne of David and over his kingdom, to establish it and to uphold it with justice and with righteousness from this time forth and forevermore. The zeal of the LORD of hosts will do this. (Is. 9:6–7)

Although Matthew introduces this quotation in chapter 4, it is evident that he sees its fulfillment as including the events recorded in chapter 28, when the resurrected Jesus appears to his disciples in Galilee (see Matt. 28:7, 10, 16). At this point, those walking in the land of the shadow of death see the light. Only with the resurrection of Jesus is Isaiah 9:1–2 truly fulfilled.

THE KINGDOM OF HEAVEN AND JEWS

Of all the Gospels, Matthew contains some of the strongest statements regarding the importance of Jesus' ministry to the Jews. Only Matthew refers to (a) Jesus and his disciples going to the lost sheep of the house of Israel (Matt. 10:5–6; 15:24) and (b) an ongoing Jewish mission (Matt. 10:23).

Alongside the Jewishness of Matthew we must also recognize that it appears to be often anti-Jewish (see Matt. 8:10–12; 21:43; 23:29–39; 27:24–25). As Professor Graham Stanton remarks, "Whereas Mark refers to the Pharisees as hypocrites only once (7:6) and Luke not at all, Matthew has twelve such references, six of which are in chapter 23."[1] Moreover, Matthew makes no reference to friendly Pharisees, in contrast to Luke (e.g., Luke 7:36; 14:1; 13:31). Matthew also associates the synagogues with the scribes and Pharisees; note how he speaks of "their synagogues" (Matt. 4:23; 9:35; 10:17; 12:9; 13:54; compare 23:34, "your synagogues").

Matthew's Gospel highlights a clear relationship between the Jewish rejection of Jesus and God's judgment upon the nation. Although Jesus enjoys the enthusiastic support of the "crowds," they do not understand fully who he is (e.g., Matt. 13:11–15); even his own disciples are slow to grasp his true identity. Later, Matthew contrasts the reaction of the Jewish pilgrims to Jesus when he enters Jerusalem (Matt. 21:1–11) with those of the temple authorities (Matt. 21:12–22:46). Significantly, in his final discourse (chs. 23–25), Jesus predicts God's judgment on the nation of Israel; the destruction of the temple is viewed in particular as an act of divine judgment (Matt. 23:37–24:20).

Yet, although Matthew's Gospel emphasizes God's judgment of the Jewish people, it does not state that God has rejected all of them forever. Various verses indicate that Jews

---

[1] G. N. Stanton, "The Communities of Matthew," *Interpretation* 46 (1992): 382.

will turn to Jesus as Messiah (Matt. 23:39; 24:30) and Jews are not excluded from the Great Commission in Matthew 28:19. Matthew 10:23 may even suggest that the Jewish mission should take priority over the Gentile mission.

THE KINGDOM OF HEAVEN AND GENTILES

In spite of its Jewishness, Matthew's Gospel has some of the strongest statements about the inclusion of Gentiles. Only Matthew has the Gentile Magi coming to honor the Christ child (Matt. 2:1–12) and only Matthew records the Great Commission (Matt. 28:19). In Matthew 8:5–13, Jesus states that "the sons of the kingdom will be thrown into the outer darkness" whereas "many will come from east and west and recline at table with Abraham, Isaac, and Jacob." This comment comes in the context of Jesus' commending the faith of a Roman centurion. Significantly, Jesus indicates that Gentiles will sit with faithful Israelites (Abraham, Isaac, and Jacob) at the banquet in the kingdom of heaven.

SUMMARY

Drawing these different strands together, Matthew's Gospel presents Jesus as the son of David, the divinely promised Messiah whose coming inaugurates the kingdom of God or heaven. In contrast to contemporary expectations, the kingdom will start small and grow gradually, consisting of everyone who acknowledges Jesus as King. Until its consummation, the righteous and the wicked will coexist. While the kingdom has no geographical limits, embracing both Jews and Gentiles, those who are in the kingdom will exhibit a lifestyle that distinguishes them from others. All of this centers on Jesus Christ, who, following his death and resurrection, receives all authority in heaven and on earth and promises to be with his disciples forever. With good reason, therefore, Matthew's Gospel may be seen as portraying Jesus as *the son of David who establishes the kingdom of heaven.*

DISCUSSION QUESTIONS

1. Matthew records that various people addressed or described Jesus as the "son of David." Focusing on Matthew 9:27–30, 12:22–23, and 15:22–28, what expectations or hopes do these individuals have concerning the "son of David"?

2. Matthew uses the phrase *kingdom of heaven* more than thirty times in his Gospel. In chapter 13, he groups together seven parables of Jesus that teach about the kingdom of heaven. What does each reveal about the kingdom, both present and future?

3. What light does Matthew 22:41–46 shed upon Jesus' understanding of the uniqueness of David's son? How does this incident challenge the Pharisees regarding their limited view of the "son of David"?

4. In Matthew's Gospel, Jesus is the "son of David" who establishes the kingdom of heaven. Especially in the light of Matthew 28:18–20, why is this belief still very relevant today?

LUKE'S GOSPEL AND THE HOLY SPIRIT

FROM OUR STUDY OF the Gospels of Mark and Matthew, we observed that whereas Mark presents Jesus as *the Son of God who suffers to ransom others*, Matthew emphasizes that Jesus is *the son of David who establishes the kingdom of heaven*. Luke adds another perspective to our picture of Jesus. Focusing on the compassion and humanity of Jesus, Luke portrays him as *the Savior of the world who seeks the lost*.

INTRODUCTION

The Gospel of Luke forms the first part of a two-volume work. The second volume is the Acts of the Apostles. The opening words of Acts highlight this connection:

> In the first book, O Theophilus, I have dealt with all that Jesus began to do and teach, until the day when he was taken up, after he had given commands through the Holy Spirit to the apostles whom he had chosen. (1:1–2)

Luke 1:1–4 also addresses an individual called Theophilus. Since the two volumes were almost certainly composed to complement each other, it is important when studying the Gospel of Luke to be aware of its special relationship with the book of Acts. Moreover, taken together, Luke and Acts form nearly one-quarter of the New Testament.

AUTHORSHIP

The earliest evidence regarding the authorship of the Gospel is unanimous in assigning it to Luke. Since Luke was not one of the twelve apostles, there must have been a good reason for associating his name with the composition of the Gospel. Support for the tradition of Lukan authorship comes from four passages in Acts where the author uses the designation "we," implying that he was a participant in the events recorded (Acts 16:10–17; 20:5–15; 21:1–18; 27:1–28:16). The final passage places the author in Rome at the time of Paul's imprisonment. From elsewhere in the New Testament it is possible to draw up a short list of some of those who were associated with Paul during his time in Rome. This list includes the following: Titus, Demas, Crescens, Jesus Justus, Epaphras, Epaphroditus, and Luke (for Luke, see Col. 4:14; 2 Tim. 4:11; Philem. v. 24). Of these possible candidates, Luke is clearly a strong candidate to be the author of Acts.

DATE OF COMPOSITION

Scholars differ in their dating of Luke–Acts. Some support an early date, about AD 60; others prefer a date of composition after the fall of Jerusalem in AD 70 and tend to place the book between AD 80 and 85. The earlier date is supported by the following line of argument. Certain significant events after AD 62 are not mentioned in the book of Acts. There is no mention of the death of Paul (AD 62), nor any allusion to the terrible persecutions carried out by Nero in AD 64. This suggests that Acts may have been composed before AD 62. If this is so for Acts, then logically Luke's Gospel must have been written somewhat earlier.

RELATIONSHIP TO MARK AND MATTHEW

About one-third of Luke's Gospel consists of material found in Mark. Luke incorporates into his account about half of

Mark's Gospel. Of the 350 verses that Luke has in common with Mark, about 50 percent use the same wording. Luke also shares some material with Matthew that is not found in Mark. About one-fifth of Luke's Gospel falls into this category. Leaving aside the material shared with Mark and Matthew, almost 50 percent of Luke's Gospel consists of material that is unique to him. Of the forty passages in the Gospels normally designated as parables, fifteen are found only in Luke.

Salvation

MAIN THEMES

In writing his Gospel, Luke displays a special interest in a number of topics or themes. In the rest of this chapter we shall explore the topics of the Holy Spirit and prayer. In our next chapter, we shall consider Luke's treatment of the important theme of salvation, alongside his interest in the despised and those of low social standing. Finally, we shall consider the related topics of joy and praise.

lost. + despised

HOLY SPIRIT

Luke is especially interested in the Holy Spirit. We are perhaps most familiar with this emphasis from the book of Acts where the coming of the Spirit on the day of Pentecost empowers the early church to proclaim boldly the good news about Jesus. However, even in Luke's Gospel much attention is given to the activity of the Spirit.

At the outset, Luke recounts the Holy Spirit's activity in the lives of different people associated with the birth of Jesus—Zechariah, Mary, Elizabeth, John, and Simeon. Prominence is given to the fact that John "will be filled with the Holy Spirit, even from his mother's womb" (Luke 1:15). Luke observes that Mary conceives Jesus by the Spirit:

And the angel answered her, "The Holy Spirit will come upon you, and the power of the Most High will overshadow you; therefore the child to be born will be called holy—the Son of God." (1:35)

A few verses later we read how Elizabeth was filled with the Holy Spirit (Luke 1:41), and soon after this Luke records that Zechariah had a similar experience:

And his father Zechariah was filled with the Holy Spirit and prophesied, saying, "Blessed be the Lord God of Israel, for he has visited and redeemed his people." (1:67–68)

The Holy Spirit is later associated with Simeon and plays a significant role in the short account concerning his encounter with the baby Jesus. Note how often the Spirit is mentioned in Luke 2:25–32:

Now there was a man in Jerusalem, whose name was Simeon, and this man was righteous and devout, waiting for the consolation of Israel, and the Holy Spirit was upon him. And it had been revealed to him by the Holy Spirit that he would not see death before he had seen the Lord's Christ. And he came in the Spirit into the temple, and when the parents brought in the child Jesus, to do for him according to the custom of the Law, he took him up in his arms and blessed God and said, "Lord, now you are letting your servant depart in peace, according to your word; for my eyes have seen your salvation that you have prepared in the presence of all peoples, a light for revelation to the Gentiles, and for glory to your people Israel."

Later, John the Baptist comments that Jesus' ministry will involve the Holy Spirit's activity:

John answered them all, saying, "I baptize you with water, but he who is mightier than I is coming, the strap of whose sandals I am not worthy to untie. He will baptize you with the Holy Spirit and with fire. His winnowing fork is in his hand, to clear his threshing floor and to gather the wheat into his barn, but the chaff he will burn with unquenchable fire." (Luke 3:16–17)

Having recorded John's comment about how the Holy Spirit will be associated with Jesus' ministry, Luke then describes briefly how Jesus himself is empowered by the Holy Spirit. At the baptism of Jesus, the Spirit comes on him:

> Now when all the people were baptized, and when Jesus also had been baptized and was praying, the heavens were opened, and the Holy Spirit descended on him in bodily form, like a dove; and a voice came from heaven, "You are my beloved Son; with you I am well pleased." (Luke 3:21–22)

Shortly after this the Holy Spirit leads Jesus into the Judean wilderness (Luke 4:1).

When Jesus begins his ministry in Galilee, according to Luke, he is very conscious of the Spirit's presence. The concept of Jesus being empowered by the Holy Spirit is highlighted when he reads from Isaiah 61:1–2 in the synagogue at Nazareth:

> And Jesus returned in the power of the Spirit to Galilee, and a report about him went out through all the surrounding country. And he taught in their synagogues, being glorified by all. And he came to Nazareth, where he had been brought up. And as was his custom, he went to the synagogue on the Sabbath day, and he stood up to read. And the scroll of the prophet Isaiah was given to him. He unrolled the scroll and found the place where it was written, "The Spirit of the Lord is upon me, because he has anointed me to proclaim good news to the poor. He has sent me to proclaim liberty to the captives and recovering of sight to the blind, to set at liberty those who are oppressed, to proclaim the year of the Lord's favor." And he rolled up the scroll and gave it back to the attendant and sat down. And the eyes of all in the synagogue

were fixed on him. And he began to say to them, "Today this Scripture has been fulfilled in your hearing." (Luke 4:14–21)

This passage is highly significant for Luke because it sets the agenda for Christ's whole ministry. For this reason he places it right at the start of his description of Jesus' ministry in Galilee. Let us note briefly three things:

- First, Jesus sees himself as fulfilling the various tasks listed in Isaiah 61:1–2. Here, as elsewhere in all four Gospels, the theme of fulfillment is important. Jesus' life has to be understood in the light of divine expectations given to earlier generations.
- Second, this passage reveals why Jesus is anointed by the Spirit. The Holy Spirit empowers him for all that he does.
- Third, Jesus' ministry will impact the poor, the captive, the blind, and the oppressed.

As Luke's account of the life of Jesus proceeds, he notes that the Holy Spirit will be active in the lives of his followers. We see this affirmed by Jesus in various passages:

If you then, who are evil, know how to give good gifts to your children, how much more will the heavenly Father give the Holy Spirit to those who ask him! (Luke 11:13)

Then he opened their minds to understand the Scriptures, and said to them, "Thus it is written, that the Christ should suffer and on the third day rise from the dead, and that repentance and forgiveness of sins should be proclaimed in his name to all nations, beginning from Jerusalem. You are witnesses of these things. And behold, I am sending the promise of my Father upon you. But stay in the city until you are clothed with power from on high." (Luke 24:45–49)

This reference to "power from on high" is developed further in Acts 1:4–8:

And while staying with them he ordered them not to depart from Jerusalem, but to wait for the promise of the Father, which, he said, "you heard from me; for John baptized with water, but you will be baptized with the Holy Spirit not many days from now." So when they had come together, they asked him, "Lord, will you at this time restore the kingdom to Israel?" He said to them, "It is not for you to know times or seasons that the Father has fixed by his own authority. But you will receive power when the Holy Spirit has come upon you, and you will be my witnesses in Jerusalem and in all Judea and Samaria, and to the end of the earth."

From this brief survey we can see that the activity of the Holy Spirit explains the source of Jesus' power. In the light of this, it is hardly surprising that the early church also was empowered by the Holy Spirit to fulfill its mission in Jesus' name.

PRAYER

A number of factors suggest that Luke has a special interest in prayer. He has nine references to Jesus praying, seven of which are unique to his Gospel (at his baptism, 3:21; 5:16; before choosing the twelve, 6:12; 9:18; at the Mount of Transfiguration, 9:28–29; 10:21–22; 11:1; at the Mount of Olives, 22:41–46; 23:46). Only Luke records that Jesus prayed for Peter:

Simon, Simon, behold, Satan demanded to have you, that he might sift you like wheat, but I have prayed for you that your faith may not fail. And when you have turned again, strengthen your brothers. (22:31–32)

Several parables provide teaching about the right kind of prayers to be offered (Luke 11:1–13; 18:1–8; 18:9–14). At the cleansing of the temple Jesus comments, "My house shall be a house of prayer" (Luke 19:46). Jesus also exhorted his followers to pray (Luke 6:28; 11:2; 22:40, 46) and warned against offering prayers that are inappropriate (Luke 20:47).

Apart from these references to prayer, Luke highlights the way in which prayer changes the lives of others. We see this, for example, in the opening chapters of Luke with regard to both Zechariah and the prophetess Anna:

> But the angel said to him, "Do not be afraid, Zechariah, for your prayer has been heard, and your wife Elizabeth will bear you a son, and you shall call his name John." (1:13)

> And there was a prophetess, Anna, the daughter of Phanuel, of the tribe of Asher. She was advanced in years, having lived with her husband seven years from when she was a virgin, and then as a widow until she was eighty-four. She did not depart from the temple, worshiping with fasting and prayer night and day. And coming up at that very hour she began to give thanks to God and to speak of him to all who were waiting for the redemption of Jerusalem. (2:36–38)

By drawing their attention to prayer in the lives of others, Luke clearly encourages his readers to pray. He continues this emphasis on prayer in the book of Acts.

In this chapter we have noted Luke's special interest in the Holy Spirit and prayer. In our next chapter we shall explore how Luke, in his portrayal of Jesus, develops the idea that he is *the Savior of the world who seeks the lost.*

DISCUSSION QUESTIONS

1. In his opening chapter, Luke underlines the activity of the Holy Spirit prior to the births of both John the Baptist and Jesus. What does this reveal about the importance of both men? How is Jesus set apart from John?

2. For Luke, Jesus' reading of Isaiah 61:1–2 in the synagogue at Nazareth is a defining moment (see Luke 4:14–21). Why is this incident so significant?

3. Luke records three parables that Jesus used to teach about prayer in 11:5–13, 18:1–8, and 18:9–14. What qualities of prayer are described? How did Jesus display these qualities in his own prayers? See Luke 5:16; 6:12; 9:28–29; 11:1–4; 22:32, 44.

4. Why does Luke give so much attention to highlighting the work of the Holy Spirit? (You may find it helpful to recall that Luke also wrote the book of Acts in which he describes the coming of the Holy Spirit at Pentecost.)

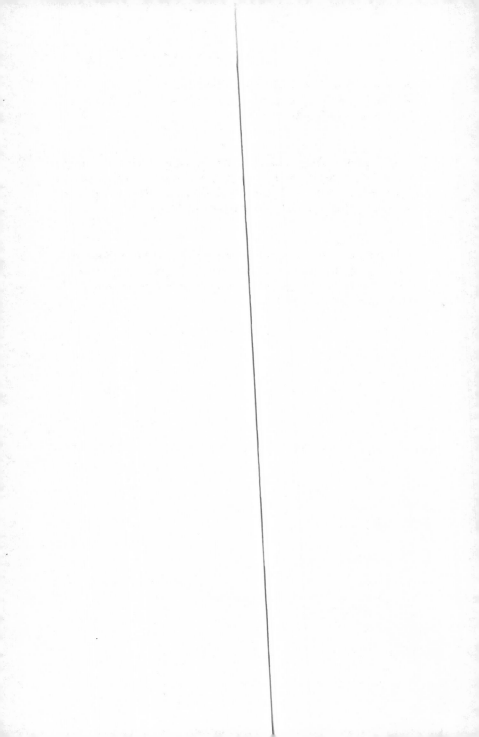

CHAPTER EIGHT

LUKE'S GOSPEL
AND SAVING THE LOST

ONE OF THE MOST striking features of Luke's Gospel is its emphasis upon the compassion of Jesus for people who were viewed as social outcasts. As we shall observe, Luke is keen to portray Jesus as *the Savior of the world who seeks the lost*. In line with this, Luke has a special interest in people. We even see this in his choice of parables. Whereas the parables of Jesus in Matthew focus on the kingdom of heaven, in Luke they are mainly people oriented.

SALVATION

Luke's Gospel highlights the concept of salvation. Words related to salvation come much more frequently in Luke's Gospel than in those of Matthew, Mark, or John. The verb "to save" appears more often in Luke than in any other book of the New Testament (*sozo* comes 15 times in Luke 6:9; 7:50; 8:12, 36, 48, 50; 9:24; 13:23; 17:19; 18:26, 42; 19:10; 23:35, 37, 39). The noun "salvation" appears six times (*soteria* comes in 1:69, 71, 77; 19:9; and *soterion* in 2:30; 3:6). Twice in his Gospel (and twice in the book of Acts) Luke uses the term *Savior*; once of God and once of Christ (Luke 1:47; 2:11). As Professor Howard Marshall rightly observes, "The central theme in the writings of Luke is that Jesus offers salvation to men [and women]."[1]

---

[1] I. H. Marshall, *Luke: Historian and Theologian* (Exeter, UK: Paternoster, 1970), 116.

By way of explaining the concept of salvation to his readers, Luke introduces the theme of seeking the lost. In three parables in chapter 15, two of which are unique to Luke, Jesus adopts illustrations about finding things that are lost—the lost sheep, the lost coin, and the lost son. Note in particular how the father celebrated when his wayward son returns home.

> And he arose and came to his father. But while he was still a long way off, his father saw him and felt compassion, and ran and embraced him and kissed him. And the son said to him, "Father, I have sinned against heaven and before you. I am no longer worthy to be called your son." But the father said to his servants, "Bring quickly the best robe, and put it on him, and put a ring on his hand, and shoes on his feet. And bring the fattened calf and kill it, and let us eat and celebrate. For this my son was dead, and is alive again; he was lost, and is found." (Luke 15:20–24)

By way of underlining Jesus' role as Savior of the lost, Luke records his encounter with Zacchaeus. Jesus' remark about Zacchaeus summarizes well the theme of salvation—"Today salvation has come to this house, since he also is a son of Abraham. For the Son of Man came to seek and to save the lost" (Luke 19:9–10).

The salvation brought by Jesus is offered to all. While Luke describes the salvation of Jews, he is especially concerned to demonstrate that this salvation is also available to Gentiles. To underline this point, Luke includes Simeon's remarks that the Christ child is "a light for revelation to the Gentiles" (Luke 2:32). In his genealogy of Jesus, Luke, unlike Matthew, traces Jesus back to Adam, the father of all humanity (Luke 3:38). When Luke quotes in 3:4–6 from Isaiah 40 he includes, unlike Matthew (3:2) and Mark (1:2–3), several more sentences, ending with the words "and all flesh shall see the salvation of God" (Luke 3:6).

In light of Jesus being the Savior of the world, Luke highlights the irony of what is said at the crucifixion of Jesus:

> And the people stood by, watching, but the rulers scoffed at him, saying, "He saved others; let him save himself, if he is the Christ of God, his Chosen One!" The soldiers also mocked him, coming up and offering him sour wine and saying, "If you are the King of the Jews, save yourself!" There was also an inscription over him, "This is the King of the Jews." One of the criminals who were hanged railed at him, saying, "Are you not the Christ? Save yourself and us!" But the other rebuked him, saying, "Do you not fear God, since you are under the same sentence of condemnation? And we indeed justly, for we are receiving the due reward of our deeds; but this man has done nothing wrong." (Luke 23:35–41)

THE DESPISED AND THOSE OF LOW SOCIAL STANDING

Luke's concern to highlight the compassion of Jesus for the lost probably explains why he has a special interest in those who were viewed as less important members of Jewish society— women, the poor, the disreputable, Samaritans, and Gentiles.

Women

Of all the Gospel writers, Luke gives the most attention to women. In his account of the infancy stories he mentions Mary, Elizabeth, and Anna. He highlights Jesus' acceptance of women by making frequent references to them (e.g., the widow of Nain [7:11–12]; the crippled woman [13:11]; the one who anoints Jesus' feet [7:37–50]). Some are even named (Mary and Martha [10:38–42]; Mary Magdalene, Joanna, and Susanna [8:2–3]). Contrary to the culture of his day Jesus encourages Mary to sit and learn. Luke alone mentions that well-to-do women funded Jesus' ministry (Luke 8:1–3). Women are placed alongside men on various occasions. In a few parables male and female pictures are set side by side (lost sheep/lost coin). A man and a woman are healed on separate Sabbaths (Luke 13:10–17; 14:1–6). In a variety of ways Luke demonstrates that women are no less important to God than men.

The Poor

The poor are important to Luke. Jesus himself was born into a poor family; the offering made at his birth reflects this (Luke 2:24; see Lev. 12:8). At the beginning of his ministry he quotes the prophecy of Isaiah that he was sent "to proclaim good news to the poor" (Luke 4:18; cf. 7:22). Jesus teaches that those who are rich must care for the poor:

> He said also to the man who had invited him, "When you give a dinner or a banquet, do not invite your friends or your brothers or your relatives or rich neighbors, lest they also invite you in return and you be repaid. But when you give a feast, invite the poor, the crippled, the lame, the blind, and you will be blessed, because they cannot repay you. For you will be repaid at the resurrection of the just." (Luke 14:12–14)

References to the poor come frequently in Luke (1:53; 6:30; 14:11–13, 21; 16:19–31; 21:1–4). To be poor is not of itself a virtue. Jesus is concerned for them because of their general helplessness and need of support.

Luke also highlights the dangers of wealth (see Luke 1:53; 6:24; 12:16–21 [the rich fool]; 16:1–12, 19–35 [the rich man and Lazarus]). The warning to the rich young ruler (Luke 18:18–27) is followed soon afterward by an account of Jesus healing a beggar (Luke 18:35–43). Next comes the story of Zacchaeus (Luke 19:1–10), which is a vivid illustration of what a rich man should do. (Later, in the book of Acts, Luke also highlights the importance of sacrificial giving in the early church [Acts 2:45; 3:6; 4:32-37; 5:1–11].)

The Disreputable

As with the poor, Luke adopts a positive outlook toward those who were viewed by others as disreputable within first-century Jewish society. He writes positively of shepherds, tax collectors, and sinners. Shepherds receive the angels' message (Luke 2:8–20). Tax collectors and sinners are at the feast given by Levi (Luke 5:30). With considerable detail Luke describes how a sinful woman washes Jesus' feet with her tears and anoints them with perfume (Luke 7:37–50):

> And behold, a woman of the city, who was a sinner, when she learned that he was reclining at table in the Pharisee's house, brought an alabaster flask of ointment, and standing behind him at his feet, weeping, she began to wet his feet with her tears and wiped them with the hair of her head and kissed his feet and anointed them with the ointment. (Luke 7:37–38)

Luke then recounts the reaction of the Pharisee who had invited Jesus to his house. When he designates the woman "a sinner," Jesus responds by telling a parable:

> And Jesus answering said to him, "Simon, I have something to say to you." And he answered, "Say it, Teacher." "A certain moneylender had two debtors. One owed five hundred denarii, and the other fifty. When they could not pay, he cancelled the debt of both. Now which of them will love him more?" Simon answered, "The one, I suppose, for whom he cancelled the larger debt." And he said to him, "You have judged rightly." Then turning toward the woman he said to Simon, "Do you see this woman? I entered your house; you gave me no water for my feet, but she has wet my feet with her tears and wiped them with her hair. You gave me no kiss, but from the time I came in she has not ceased to kiss my feet. You did not anoint my head with oil, but she has anointed my feet with ointment. Therefore I tell you, her sins, which are many, are forgiven—for she loved much. But he who is forgiven little,

loves little." And he said to her, "Your sins are forgiven."
Then those who were at table with him began to say among
themselves, "Who is this, who even forgives sins?" And
he said to the woman, "Your faith has saved you; go in
peace." (Luke 7:40–50)

With remarkable boldness Jesus contrasts the love and
affection of the "sinful" woman with that of his host, a
Pharisee. Later, in a parable that is unique to Luke, Jesus contrasts a tax collector and a self-righteous Pharisee when they
go to the temple to pray (Luke 18:9–14). Of the two men,
according to Jesus, only the repentant tax collector comes
away forgiven by God.

Samaritans and Gentiles
Luke alone has the stories of the good man from Samaria
(Luke 10:25–37) and the healing of the ten lepers when only
a Samaritan returns to give thanks (Luke 17:11–19). Certain
Gentiles are portrayed in a favorable light in this Gospel—the
widow of Zarephath and Naaman the Syrian (Luke 4:25–27).
Luke draws attention to the idea that Israel's rejection of Jesus
will be accompanied by the Gentiles' receiving him favorably.
This theme is developed at the end of Luke:

Then he opened their minds to understand the Scriptures,
and said to them, "Thus it is written, that the Christ should
suffer and on the third day rise from the dead, and that
repentance and forgiveness of sins should be proclaimed
in his name to all nations, beginning from Jerusalem."
(24:45–47)

Luke's second volume, the book of Acts, develops fur-
ther the theme of the salvation of the Gentiles. In Acts,
Luke describes in detail how the church expands from
Jerusalem in Judea to Samaria and then to the Gentile world.

Interestingly, on each occasion there is a new outpouring of the Holy Spirit.

JOY AND PRAISE

Knowledge of the Savior of the world should lead to rejoicing. Consequently, joy and praise are important throughout Luke's Gospel. In the infancy accounts he records a number of great hymns—the angels' song (Luke 2:14), the Magnificat (Luke 1:46–55), the Benedictus (Luke 1:68–79), and the Nunc Dimittis (Luke 2:29–32). People praise or glorify God (Luke 2:20; 5:25–26; 7:16; 13:13; 17:15; 18:43). There is joy over the lost sheep (Luke 15:6–7), the lost coin (Luke 15:9–10), and the lost son (Luke 15:23–25, 32). There is joy when Zacchaeus receives Jesus (Luke 19:6). The Gospel even ends on a note of praise—"And they were continually in the temple blessing God" (Luke 24:20).

As these examples illustrate, Luke undoubtedly weaves into his Gospel the theme of joy and praise because this is the appropriate response to the good news that Jesus has come as *the Savior of the world to seek the lost.*

DISCUSSION QUESTIONS

1. What is the main thrust of the parables of the lost sheep and the lost coin in Luke 15? Why does Luke place these two parables together, followed by a third about a "lost" son?

2. As the "Son of Man," Jesus expresses concern for many people. What is striking about the individuals mentioned in the following passages? See Luke 5:29–32; 7:11–16; 8:1–3, 41–56; 10:38–42; 13:10–17; 18:15–17; 23:39–43. How do these passages relate to Jesus' mission statement recorded in Luke 19:10?

3. What do we mean when we say that we are saved? How would you describe "salvation" as it applies to your daily life? In the light of Luke 10:25–37, what does it means to be an "authentic disciple" of Jesus in today's world?

4. How does the story of Zacchaeus illustrate well some of the main themes of Luke's Gospel?

CHAPTER NINE

JOHN'S GOSPEL AND BELIEVING

ALTHOUGH THE GOSPELS OF Mark, Matthew, and Luke share much in common, each gives a different perspective on Jesus Christ. Mark stresses that Jesus is *the Son of God who suffers to ransom others*. Matthew focuses on the concept of Jesus as *the son of David who establishes the kingdom of heaven*. Luke emphasizes the compassion and humanity of Jesus as *the Savior of the world who seeks the lost*. With John's Gospel, it is more difficult to isolate one theme that captures his particular emphasis concerning Jesus. Among various options we shall concentrate on the idea that Jesus is presented as *the Lamb of God who brings eternal life through a new exodus*.

AUTHOR

Most scholars accept that the internal evidence points toward the author of the fourth Gospel as being a Jew from Palestine. The book displays a knowledge of the region, its customs, and its language. The evidence from the early church points to the author as being the apostle John, one of the sons of Zebedee. Irenaeus, writing at the end of the second century, refers to a statement by Polycarp (martyred in AD 156) that he had met the apostle John and listened to his account of the miracles and teaching of Jesus. Irenaeus elsewhere writes, "John the disciple of the LORD, who leaned back on his breast, published the

Gospel while he was resident at Ephesus in Asia" (*Adv. Haer.* 2.1.2*). The comment about the disciple leaning back on Jesus' breast is probably a reference to the beloved disciple of John 13:23.

The author appears to be this "beloved disciple," mentioned on various occasions in John's Gospel. He is first referred to in John 13:23 at the Last Supper, where he is found reclining next to Jesus. He appears again at the time of the crucifixion when Jesus instructs him to take care of Mary (John 19:26–27). He accompanies Peter to the empty tomb (John 20:2–9) and, although he arrives first, he lets Peter enter before him. In chapter 21 there is a further reference to the beloved disciple (John 21:20–24):

> Peter turned and saw the disciple whom Jesus loved following them, the one who had been reclining at table close to him and had said, "Lord, who is it that is going to betray you?" When Peter saw him, he said to Jesus, "Lord, what about this man?" Jesus said to him, "If it is my will that he remain until I come, what is that to you? You follow me!" So the saying spread abroad among the brothers that this disciple was not to die; yet Jesus did not say to him that he was not to die, but, "If it is my will that he remain until I come, what is that to you?" This is the disciple who is bearing witness about these things, and who has written these things, and we know that his testimony is true.

On the basis of this passage it is inferred that the beloved disciple wrote the entire Gospel. (However, "these things" might not refer to the whole book, making it also possible that the disciple of verse 24 was not the beloved disciple.)

Traditionally the beloved disciple has been identified as the apostle John, the son of Zebedee. The following evidence is adduced. First, he has to be one of the twelve; only the apostles shared in the Last Supper (Mark 14:17). Second, he is always distinguished from Peter (John 13:23–24; 20:2–9; 21:20) and is sometimes found accompanying Peter. According to the Synoptic Gospels, the book of Acts, and Galatians, Peter and John were close companions (Mark 5:37; 9:2; 14:33; Acts 3:1–4:23; 8:15–25; Galatians 2:9). Third, he appears to be one of those who go fishing in 21:2–3. These include Peter, Thomas, Nathanael, the sons of Zebedee, and two other disciples. He cannot be James, the brother of John, since James was martyred during the reign of Herod Agrippa I (AD 41–44; see Acts 12:1–2), and the beloved disciple appears to have lived for a long time (John 21:23). Fourth, neither James nor John, the sons of Zebedee, are ever named in the fourth Gospel, a strange omission given the number of others specifically named. This might not appear so peculiar if John was the author. Last, whereas most people in the fourth Gospel are given their full names (e.g., Simon Peter; Thomas Didymus; Judas, son of Iscariot), this is not so for John the Baptist; he is merely referred to as John (e.g., 1:6). It is suggested that only John, the son of Zebedee, would not feel it necessary to distinguish John the Baptist from himself.

THE DIFFERENCES BETWEEN JOHN AND THE SYNOPTIC GOSPELS

The Gospel of John differs from the Synoptic Gospels in a number of ways. Many events that play an important role in the Synoptic Gospels are absent—the baptism of Jesus, the call of the Twelve, the transfiguration, and the institution of the Lord's Supper. John also has no exorcisms and noticeably fewer parables. Indeed, John's Gospel does not use the term "parable" although it appears forty-eight times in the Synoptic Gospels.

John does not adopt the geographical-chronological structure that is so apparent in the Synoptic Gospels. Although John connects Jesus with Galilee, this is not emphasized greatly. John concentrates more on Jesus' time in Jerusalem. Consequently, unlike Mark and the other Synoptic Gospels, John records three journeys by Jesus to Jerusalem in order to celebrate Jewish festivals (John 2:13; 5:1; 7:10).

The first five chapters of John have only two passages that focus on events in Galilee (John 2:1–11 and 4:43–54). On the first occasion Jesus changes water into wine, and on the second occasion he heals the son of a royal official. Both events are viewed as signs:

> This, the first of his signs, Jesus did at Cana in Galilee, and manifested his glory. And his disciples believed in him. (John 2:11)

> This was now the second sign that Jesus did when he had come from Judea to Galilee. (John 4:54)

John notes that these were the first and second "signs" performed by Jesus in Galilee. Between these events, Jesus travels to Jerusalem where he meets Nicodemus. Then on his journey back to Galilee he encounters the woman at a well in Samaria. After the second sign, in chapter 5 Jesus returns to Jerusalem where he heals a lame man on the Sabbath.

John also differs from the Synoptic Gospels by having fewer, longer episodes. Individual scenes are described in more detail, with special attention being given to conversations. The first half of the Gospel is dominated by dialogues between Jesus and a handful of individuals (e.g., Nicodemus [ch. 3], the woman of Samaria [ch. 4], the man who was ill for thirty-eight years [ch. 5], and the man born blind [ch. 9]). None of these people appears in the Synoptic Gospels. In chapters 13–17, the Gospel records at length Jesus' interaction with his disciples at the Last

Supper. Again, John's account is quite different from that found in the Synoptic Gospels.

STRUCTURE

By abandoning the geographical-chronological structure of the Synoptic Gospels, John has freedom to shape his account in a very different way. Consequently, the structure of John's Gospel is unique. It is perhaps easiest to view John's Gospel as falling into two halves, apart from an introductory prologue and concluding epilogue.

CHART 9.1

John

| Introduction 1 | Seven Signs and Discourses 2–11 | Passion Narrative 12–19 | Resurrection 20–21 |

The first half of the Gospel is dominated by two features. First, John draws attention to seven signs (or miracles). These move from the changing of water into wine through to the resurrection of Lazarus. Second, John records a number of dialogues between Jesus and a handful of individuals. The second half of the Gospel is taken up with the events surrounding the crucifixion of Jesus. Chapters 13–17 chiefly report a long discourse and prayer by Jesus.

Although the two halves of John's Gospel are quite distinct as regards their content, they are carefully tied together by the final verses of chapter 11. This bridging passage links the signs of Jesus to his eventual death:

> So the chief priests and the Pharisees gathered the Council and said, "What are we to do? For this man performs many signs. If we let him go on like this, everyone will believe in

him, and the Romans will come and take away both our place and our nation." But one of them, Caiaphas, who was high priest that year, said to them, "You know nothing at all. Nor do you understand that it is better for you that one man should die for the people, not that the whole nation should perish." He did not say this of his own accord, but being high priest that year he prophesied that Jesus would die for the nation, and not for the nation only, but also to gather into one the children of God who are scattered abroad. So from that day on they made plans to put him to death. (John 11:47–53)

Building on what has been recorded in the preceding chapters, these verses anticipate the events that are about to unfold.

MAIN THEMES

There is a richness to John's Gospel that makes it difficult to encapsulate all of his ideas by picking out only a few main themes. We shall explore two themes which we hope will embrace much of what John says. These are—believing and a new exodus. The latter of these will be discussed in our next chapter.

Believing

There can be little doubt that the theme of believing is important to John. The Greek verb *pisteuo* "to believe" comes a total of ninety-eight times in John's Gospel. This represents just over one-quarter of all the occurrences in the New Testament. The importance of "believing" is captured well in the passage that concerns "Doubting Thomas":

So the other disciples told him, "We have seen the Lord." But he said to them, "Unless I see in his hands the mark of the nails, and place my finger into the mark of the nails, and place my hand into his side, I will never believe." Eight days later, his disciples were inside again, and Thomas was with them. Although the doors were locked, Jesus came and stood among them and said, "Peace be with you." Then he said to

Thomas, "Put your finger here, and see my hands; and put out your hand, and place it in my side. Do not disbelieve, but believe." Thomas answered him, "My Lord and my God!" Jesus said to him, "Have you believed because you have seen me? Blessed are those who have not seen and yet have believed." Now Jesus did many other signs in the presence of the disciples, which are not written in this book; but these are written so that you may believe that Jesus is the Christ, the Son of God, and that by believing you may have life in his name. (John 20:25–31)

John clearly wants to encourage his readers to believe that Jesus is the Christ, the Son of God.

Christ

John 20:30–31 explains briefly why John wrote his Gospel. The first purpose clause in verse 31 ought to be rendered "that you may believe that the Christ, the Son of God, is Jesus." The fourth Gospel answers the question, "Who is the Messiah?" not, "Who is Jesus?" This draws attention to the evangelistic purpose of the book. It appears to have been written for Jews of the Diaspora (that is, the region outside the land of Israel) and Jewish proselytes (that is, Gentiles who converted to Judaism) and seeks to convince them that the Messiah is Jesus. A number of passages in John underline this point:

He [Andrew] first found his own brother Simon and said to him, "We have found the Messiah" (which means Christ). (1:41)

When they heard these words, some of the people said, "This really is the Prophet." Others said, "This is the Christ." But some said, "Is the Christ to come from Galilee? Has not the Scripture said that the Christ comes from the offspring of David, and comes from Bethlehem, the village where David was?" So there was a division among the people over him. (7:40–43)

> His parents said these things because they feared the Jews, for the Jews had already agreed that if anyone should confess Jesus to be Christ, he was to be put out of the synagogue. (9:22)

> Jesus said to her, "I am the resurrection and the life. Whoever believes in me, though he die, yet shall he live, and everyone who lives and believes in me shall never die. Do you believe this?" She said to him, "Yes, Lord; I believe that you are the Christ, the Son of God, who is coming into the world." (11:25–27)

Apart from claiming that Jesus is the Christ or Messiah, John's Gospel draws attention to Jesus' status as the Son of God.

Son of God

John emphasizes that Jesus is the Son of God. This is the most important title for Jesus in John's Gospel, a point underlined by the fact that he uses the word "father" 137 times, mostly with reference to God. John spells out the special way in which the Father and the Son are related. With perfect obedience Jesus does everything that the Father requires (John 5:19–47). As the only Son, Jesus makes known (better "interprets") the Father for he is God's Word to humanity. Moreover, the Father sends his Son to be Savior of the world (John 3:16).

Something of the intimate connection between the Father and the Son is captured in 3:34–36:

> For he whom God has sent utters the words of God, for he gives the Spirit without measure. The Father loves the Son and has given all things into his hand. Whoever believes in the Son has eternal life; whoever does not obey the Son shall not see life, but the wrath of God remains on him.

By underlining the special relationship between the Father and the Son, John encourages his readers to place their trust in Jesus. As we shall see in our next chapter, John presents Jesus as bringing about a new exodus, through which his followers receive eternal life.

DISCUSSION QUESTIONS

1. John's Gospel does not share the family characteristics of the other three Gospels. Summarize briefly the main ways in which John's account of Jesus' life differs from the others.

2. John emphasizes that Jesus brings eternal life. How do the seven "signs" recorded by John support this idea?

3. John introduces his reason for writing the Gospel by relating the story of "Doubting Thomas" (John 20:24–31). Why do you think he chose this particular incident?

4. Eternal life does not mean that we shall continue to live in this world forever. What light does John 14:1–3 shed on the nature of eternal life? How can this passage offer us reassurance about the future?

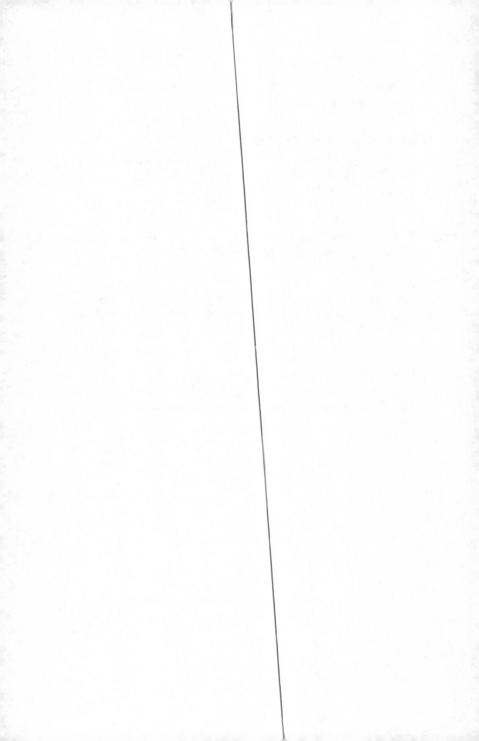

CHAPTER TEN

JOHN'S GOSPEL
AND A NEW EXODUS

WHEN READING JOHN'S GOSPEL it is important to realize that it contains a large number of allusions to the Old Testament. In the main, John's method of linking Jesus to the Old Testament differs from that of the Synoptic Gospels, although they all share the common belief that Jesus brings to fulfillment important Old Testament expectations.

Complementing the other Gospels, John sees the life, death, and resurrection of Jesus as initiating a "new exodus." At the heart of this belief is the idea that the death of Jesus is the ultimate Passover sacrifice. To appreciate how John presents Jesus as *the Lamb of God who brings eternal life through a new exodus*, we need to observe that his entire Gospel develops concepts closely associated with the Old Testament book of Exodus. Three elements are particularly noteworthy—signs, feasts, and the "I am" sayings.

SIGNS

Omitting the resurrection of Jesus, John records seven signs, all in chapters 2–11 and dominating the first half of the Gospel.

1. 2:2–11   Water to wine
2. 4:46–54   Healing of an official's son
3. 5:1–15   Healing of a paralyzed man

4. 6:1–14   Feeding of five thousand
5. 6:15–21   Walking on water
6. 9:1–41   Healing of a blind man
7. 11:1–45   Raising of Lazarus

There are several observations to be made about these signs. First, John draws attention to the fact that the signs performed by Jesus enable people to believe:

> This, the first of his signs, Jesus did at Cana in Galilee, and manifested his glory. And his disciples believed in him. (2:11)

> Now when he was in Jerusalem at the Passover Feast, many believed in his name when they saw the signs that he was doing. (2:23)

Jesus himself makes the point that without "signs" the people will not believe:

> So Jesus said to him, "Unless you see signs and wonders you will not believe." (John 4:48)

This point is echoed later when John briefly explains the purpose behind the writing of his Gospel:

> Now Jesus did many other signs in the presence of the disciples, which are not written in this book; but these are written so that you may believe that Jesus is the Christ, the Son of God, and that by believing you may have life in his name. (20:30–31)

Second, these signs are viewed as revealing that Jesus is God's chosen, anointed one:

> Yet many of the people believed in him. They said, "When the Christ appears, will he do more signs than this man has done?" (John 7:31)

Some of the Pharisees said, "This man is not from God, for he does not keep the Sabbath." But others said, "How can a man who is a sinner do such signs?" And there was a division among them. (John 9:16)

Third, these signs parallel various "signs" in the book of Exodus. God gave signs to Moses in order to convince others that he had come from God. We read about this in Exodus 4:1–9:

> Then Moses answered, "But behold, they will not believe me or listen to my voice, for they will say, 'The LORD did not appear to you.'" The LORD said to him, "What is that in your hand?" He said, "A staff." And he said, "Throw it on the ground." So he threw it on the ground, and it became a serpent, and Moses ran from it. But the LORD said to Moses, "Put out your hand and catch it by the tail"—so he put out his hand and caught it, and it became a staff in his hand—"that they may believe that the LORD, the God of their fathers, the God of Abraham, the God of Isaac, and the God of Jacob, has appeared to you." Again, the LORD said to him, "Put your hand inside your cloak." And he put his hand inside his cloak, and when he took it out, behold, his hand was leprous like snow. Then God said, "Put your hand back inside your cloak." So he put his hand back inside his cloak, and when he took it out, behold, it was restored like the rest of his flesh. "If they will not believe you," God said, "or listen to the first sign, they may believe the latter sign. If they will not believe even these two signs or listen to your voice, you shall take some water from the Nile and pour it on the dry ground, and the water that you shall take from the Nile will become blood on the dry ground."

Later, when Moses performed these signs before the Israelites, they believed:

> Then Moses and Aaron went and gathered together all the elders of the people of Israel. Aaron spoke all the words that

the LORD had spoken to Moses and did the signs in the sight of the people. And the people believed; and when they heard that the LORD had visited the people of Israel and that he had seen their affliction, they bowed their heads and worshiped. (Ex. 4:29–31)

Interestingly, however, when Moses performed the same signs before Pharaoh and the Egyptians, they did not believe. However, when God sends further signs the Egyptians gradually believe, even though Pharaoh does so very reluctantly. While we usually refer to the events that took place in Egypt as plagues, the book of Exodus refers to them more often as "signs" and "wonders."

Undoubtedly, we are meant to see a connection between the signs in Egypt and those performed by Jesus. Yet, whereas the former are signs of judgment, the latter are signs of hope. In Egypt water is turned into blood; in Cana water is turned into wine. In Exodus the final sign is the death of firstborn males; in John the final sign is the resurrection of Lazarus. As the signs in Exodus prepare the way for an exodus from Egypt, bringing a new life to enslaved people, so, too, in the Gospel of John. The signs performed by Jesus anticipate a new exodus through which Jesus brings eternal life to those who are enslaved by evil.

FEASTS

The second major feature of John's Gospel that associates it with the book of Exodus is the prominence given to religious feasts or festivals. John's Gospel gives special attention to three Passovers (John 2:13; 6:4; 11:55) and mentions several other feasts. Significantly, the oldest Jewish feasts (Passover and Unleavened Bread, Weeks, and Booths) all celebrated different aspects of the Israelites' deliverance from Egypt.

Of particular importance is the Passover itself. Much is

made of the fact that the death of Jesus occurred at the Passover. Indeed, John underlines that Jesus' death parallels the death of the Passover lamb or kid because his bones were not broken:

> Since it was the day of Preparation, and so that the bodies would not remain on the cross on the Sabbath (for that Sabbath was a high day), the Jews asked Pilate that their legs might be broken and that they might be taken away. So the soldiers came and broke the legs of the first, and of the other who had been crucified with him. But when they came to Jesus and saw that he was already dead, they did not break his legs. But one of the soldiers pierced his side with a spear, and at once there came out blood and water. He who saw it has borne witness—his testimony is true, and he knows that he is telling the truth—that you also may believe. For these things took place that the Scripture might be fulfilled: "Not one of his bones will be broken." (19:31–36)

The short biblical quotation at the end of this passage echoes Exodus 12:46 and refers to the bones of the Passover sacrifice:

> It shall be eaten in one house; you shall not take any of the flesh outside the house, and you shall not break any of its bones.

John evidently sees the timing and manner of Jesus' death as significant. Jesus' death is understood to be a Passover sacrifice. Interestingly, earlier in the Gospel, John the Baptist introduces Jesus as the "Lamb of God, who takes away the sin of the world" (John 1:29; cf. 1:36). John, the author of the Gospel, sees this being fulfilled when Jesus is crucified at Passover.

I AM

Another very distinctive feature of John's Gospel is Jesus' use of the expression "I am," often used with a predicate:

- I am the bread of life (John 6:35)
- I am the light of the world (John 8:12)
- I am the door (John 10:7, 9)
- I am the good shepherd (John 10:11)
- I am the resurrection and the life (John 11:25)
- I am the way, and the truth, and the life (John 14:6)
- I am the true vine (John 15:1)

All of these remarkable claims by Jesus are only found in John's Gospel. Elsewhere, Jesus sometimes uses "I am" without a predicate (John 8:24, 28, 58; 13:19). On such occasions the expression "I am" is clearly viewed as significant. We see this, for example, in John 8:57–59:

> So the Jews said to him, "You are not yet fifty years old, and have you seen Abraham?" Jesus said to them, "Truly, truly, I say to you, before Abraham was, I am." So they picked up stones to throw at him, but Jesus hid himself and went out of the temple.

Evidently, Jesus' use of "I am" was viewed as blasphemous, no doubt because it was thought to echo Exodus 3:14. In Exodus 3 God introduces himself to Moses using the phrase "I am":

> God said to Moses, "I AM WHO I AM." And he said, "Say this to the people of Israel, 'I AM has sent me to you.'" (14)

By claiming to be "I am," Jesus placed himself on par with God. For this reason, some of those listening wanted to stone Jesus.

A NEW EXODUS

Why does John's Gospel give prominence to signs, feasts, and the "I am" sayings? In the Old Testament, the exodus of the Israelites from oppression in Egypt was the great event of divine deliverance. Each year it was remembered through the different festivals and especially through the partial re-enactment of the original Passover, leading into the seven-day festival of Unleavened Bread. In John's Gospel, the coming of Jesus is presented as bringing about a new and greater exodus.

Whereas the exodus from Egypt offered a new life to the Israelite slaves, the death of Jesus brings eternal life to those who believe. Various passages in John stress this idea:

> And as Moses lifted up the serpent in the wilderness, so must the Son of Man be lifted up, that whoever believes in him may have eternal life. For God so loved the world, that he gave his only Son, that whoever believes in him should not perish but have eternal life. (3:14–16)

> For this is the will of my Father, that everyone who looks on the Son and believes in him should have eternal life, and I will raise him up on the last day. (6:40)

Elsewhere, Jesus reassures his disciples that their future lives are secure because of who he is:

> "Let not your hearts be troubled. Believe in God; believe also in me. In my Father's house are many rooms. If it were not so, would I have told you that I go to prepare a place for you? And if I go and prepare a place for you, I will come again and will take you to myself, that where I am you may be also. And you know the way to where I am going." Thomas said to him, "Lord, we do not know where you are going. How can we know the way?" Jesus said to him, "I am the way, and the truth, and the life. No one comes to the Father except through me." (John 14:1–6)

Through trusting in Jesus, his followers will experience eternal life. Building on this, the Gospel of John underlines the importance of continuing to believe. This is brought out in a most interesting way in chapter 6. Here we have a very rare example of John describing an event that is recorded also in the Synoptic Gospels. Like Matthew, Mark, and Luke, John narrates how Jesus feeds five thousand people. John's account, however, has something extra, not found in the Synoptics. He briefly notes that the feast of Passover was near (John 6:4) and that Jesus tested Philip (John 6:5–6). John then develops the account of the feeding of the five thousand by focusing on Jesus as the bread of life. Remarkably, this results in the Jews' and some of his disciples' murmuring about Jesus.

Striking parallels exist between John 6 and Exodus 16 where the themes of testing, bread from heaven, and grumbling or murmuring are also found. John obviously sees a connection between the Old Testament account of the exodus and the events surrounding the feeding of the five thousand.

As we discovered in the Synoptic Gospels, people often stumble when they are challenged to appreciate the truth about Jesus. Taken together, the Gospels present four remarkable portraits of Jesus. The claims that they make about this unique individual are incredible. If true, Jesus stands apart from every other human being who has walked upon the earth. The challenge for each of us is very clear. Do I believe, or will I, like some of Jesus' disciples in John 6, turn back?

DISCUSSION QUESTIONS

1. John draws attention to seven signs (miracles) performed by Jesus. How do these signs function like those given to Moses in Exodus? What is the main difference between the signs in Exodus and the signs in John?

2. John's Gospel gives prominence to signs, feasts, and the "I am" sayings. How do these features relate to Jesus' being the "Lamb of God" (John 1:29, 36)? What is the significance of Jesus' being called the "Lamb of God"?

3. John presents Jesus as the Lamb of God who brings eternal life through a new exodus. How is this relevant for today? What difference should this message make in how we live?

4. We cannot have Christianity without the cross; it is the most vital part of our faith. Imagine being asked about this by someone who does not understand the death of our Lord. How would you explain the significance of Jesus' death?

CHAPTER ELEVEN

THE COMPOSITION OF
THE GOSPELS

PENNED ALMOST two thousand years ago, the four Gospels
appear to have been composed through a process that involved
three stages. First, there was the oral stage; second, the production of substantial written accounts of the life and teaching of
Jesus; third, the production of the Gospels as we now know
them. These three stages are possibly reflected in the opening
verses of Luke's Gospel:

> Inasmuch as many have undertaken to compile a narrative
> of the things that have been accomplished among us, just
> as those who from the beginning were eyewitnesses and
> ministers of the word have delivered them to us, it seemed
> good to me also, having followed all things closely for some
> time past, to write an orderly account for you, most excel-
> lent Theophilus, that you may have certainty concerning the
> things you have been taught. (1:1–4)

Luke mentions (1) eyewitnesses; (2) the many who have
drawn up an account of the things that have been accomplished
among us; (3) the orderly account which he has produced. The
length of the oral phase of this process is usually believed to have
lasted at most twenty years (if Mark was composed about AD 55)
or possibly thirty-five years (if Mark was composed about AD 70
as some scholars suggest). However, we have no direct knowledge
of what happened in this early period. It is quite possible that
written records of what Jesus said and did may have been made
during his lifetime.

The process by which the Gospels were composed has attracted considerable attention due to the striking similarities between the Gospels of Matthew, Mark, and Luke. The close relationship between these three Gospels requires an explanation. This issue is often referred to as the Synoptic Problem.

THE SYNOPTIC PROBLEM

The term *Synoptic* was first used in relation to the Gospels by Johann Griesbach at the end of the eighteenth century. The Greek word *sunopsis* means "seeing together" and is used to designate the Gospels of Matthew, Mark, and Luke because they have a common way of seeing the life of Jesus. We can observe this "seeing together" in a number of ways.

First, Matthew, Mark, and Luke adopt the same geographic sequence in describing the adult life of Jesus—ministry in Galilee, withdrawal to the North, ministry in Judea and Perea as Jesus is on the way to Jerusalem, and finally, the events surrounding Jesus' death in Jerusalem. Second, there are many passages which are remarkably similar in the three Synoptic Gospels. Observe the close parallels between Matthew 9:6, Mark 2:10–11, and Luke 5:24.

CHART 11.1

Matthew 9:6	Mark 2:10–11	Luke 5:24
"But that you may know that the Son of Man has authority on earth to forgive sins"—he then said to the paralytic—"Rise, pick up your bed and go home."	"But that you may know that the Son of Man has authority on earth to forgive sins"—he said to the paralytic—"I say to you, rise, pick up your bed, and go home."	"But that you may know that the Son of Man has authority on earth to forgive sins"—he said to the man who was paralyzed—"I say to you, rise, pick up your bed and go home."

Not only is the wording in these verses almost exactly identical, but all three authors insert a break at the same point in the words of Jesus. However, differences also exist. Matthew omits, "I say to you," found in both Mark and Luke. In reporting the whole incident Matthew does not tell us that the man's friends opened a hole in the roof in order to let the paralyzed man down before Jesus.

Third, various statistics underline the special relationship that exists between the Synoptic Gospels. About 90 percent of Mark is found in Matthew. Of the 661 verses in Mark, more than 600 come in Matthew; of these about half are identical with regard to the actual wording. About 50 percent of Mark is found in Luke. Of the 350 verses shared by Mark and Luke, about half use the same wording. Only four paragraphs (or about forty verses) of Mark do not appear in either Matthew or Luke (Mark 4:26–29; 7:32–37; 8:22–26; 14:51–52).

Apart from their links with Mark, there are about 250 verses, not found in Mark, that are shared by Matthew and Luke. The Beatitudes and the Lord's Prayer are part of this material. How do we explain the fact that 20 percent of Matthew's Gospel is shared with Luke, but not Mark? Many scholars believe that these verses came from a document, no longer extant, consisting largely of the collected sayings of Jesus. This hypothetical document is known by scholars as Q (a label which appears to be derived from the German *Quelle*, "source"). Q contains, among other things, much of the material that is found in Matthew's Sermon on the Mount and Luke's Sermon on the Plain. All of this evidence points to some form of sharing with regard to the process by which the Synoptic Gospels were composed. How do we best account for this?

Various theories have been proposed to explain the process by which the Synoptic Gospels were composed. Most of these are based on the concept of literary dependency. To explain passages that are word-for-word the same, some form of literary borrowing seems to be the most likely explanation. (We should, however, in the light of some recent research, bear in mind the possibility of oral dependency. It is possible that some stories were communicated orally with very special attention being given to preserving their exact form and wording.)

Assuming literary dependency, two theories have dominated scholarly explanations of the Synoptic Problem. Both of these are based on the following observations:

- Matthew is often similar to Mark.
- Luke is often similar to Mark.
- Matthew and Luke, where they duplicate Mark, are rarely similar against Mark.

There are two main ways of explaining these features. On the one hand, it is possible that Mark's Gospel was penned first, and the others borrow from it.

CHART 11.2

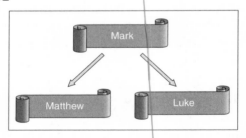

On the other hand, Mark was composed last as a digest of both Matthew and Luke.

THE TWO-SOURCE HYPOTHESIS
(MARK *BEFORE* MATTHEW AND LUKE)

The first of these explanations is known as the "two-source" or "two-document" hypothesis. It gets this name because Matthew and Luke had before them two sources—Mark and Q. First proposed by Karl Lachmann in 1835, this theory was almost universally accepted by the beginning of the twentieth century. Various considerations lend support to this view. Professor Graham Stanton lists three main reasons for Markan priority:

1. It is easy to suggest why Matthew and Luke might wish to expand Mark; it is more difficult to explain why Mark should abbreviate Matthew. Why would Mark leave out almost all of the Sermon on the Mount, yet find space to expand Matthew's narrative material (compare Mark 1:29–31 with Matthew 8:14–15)? Put more bluntly, if Matthew (and Luke) already existed, why was it necessary to produce Mark's Gospel? Almost all of Mark (90 percent) is found in Matthew.

2. Matthew and Luke often modify or omit redundant phrases in Mark to improve his rather unsophisticated literary style. In Mark 1:32 we read: "That evening at sundown. . . ." Matthew 8:16 uses the first phrase; Luke 4:40 records only the second.

3. Matthew and Luke modify a number of passages in Mark which could be understood as casting Jesus in a poor light. The phrase "is out of his mind" in Mark 3:21 is omitted in Matthew and Luke. Mark 4:38 records that the disciples asked, "Teacher, do you not care that we are perishing?" The parallel verses in Matthew 8:25 and Luke 8:24 omit "do you not care?" [1]

THE TWO-GOSPEL HYPOTHESIS (MARK *AFTER* MATTHEW AND LUKE)

The idea that Mark was composed after Matthew and Luke is sometimes referred to as the Griesbach hypothesis or "two-gospel" hypothesis. In 1789, Johann Griesbach argued for the priority of Matthew and Luke, with Mark being a later condensation of them. This supports the early Christian tradition that Matthew's Gospel was the first to be written, with Luke being

---

[1] Graham N. Stanton, *The Gospels and Jesus*, Oxford Bible Series (Oxford: Oxford University Press, 1989), 35–37.

dependent upon Matthew, and Mark being an abbreviation of both Matthew and Luke.

Against this theory, however, it is argued that Mark is unlikely to have reworked the longer accounts of Matthew and Luke and yet have produced "a condensation that is graphic, forceful, and not artificial."[2] Also, it should be noted, that although Mark is overall much shorter than Matthew, where the two Gospels contain common material, Matthew always contains the shorter version. Matthew boils down the stories in Mark to their bare essentials. For example, events that are narrated in forty-three verses in Mark 5 take up only sixteen verses in Matthew 8:28–34, and 9:18–26. Matthew's Gospel is only longer than Mark because of the additional material that it contains. And why would Mark omit so much of the teaching of Jesus, especially something as important as the Lord's Prayer? Why also would Mark retain so little material supporting the resurrection of Jesus?

While most scholars believe that the weight of evidence favors the priority of Mark's Gospel, this solution is not without problems. According to Professor Leon Morris, "It seems to me not only that have we not solved the Synoptic Problem, but also that we are not likely ever to solve it. Too much of the writing of the early church has perished."[3]

Although it is interesting to consider the way in which the Gospels were composed, we can still read and understand them without knowing the precise details of how they were produced. What is of special interest is the way in which the different authors handle all of the material at their disposal. Fortunately, we can largely observe these features without having to unravel the complex process by which the Gospels were written.

---

[2] D. A. Carson, *Matthew*, The Expositor's Bible Commentary, vol. 8, ed. F. E. Gaebelein (Grand Rapids: Zondervan, 1984), 14.
[3] L. Morris, *The Gospel According to Matthew* (Grand Rapids: Eerdmans, 1992), 17.

DIFFERENT IDEAS ABOUT THE GOSPELS

Over the past two hundred years the Gospels have been viewed in four different ways—as biographies, proclamations, distinctive theologies, and stories.

Biographies

Up to and during the nineteenth century the Gospels were viewed largely as historically reliable records. They were taken to be biographies that provided an accurate picture of Jesus Christ. However, scholars examining the Gospels did not always come up with the same picture of Jesus, and their portraits are often conditioned by other factors. For example, nineteenth-century accounts of the life of Jesus tend to portray him as a Victorian gentleman.

Proclamations

As a reaction against the idea that the Gospels are simply biographies, some scholars have favored the idea that they are proclamations. Those adopting this outlook believe that much of the material in the Gospels was shaped by the early church as part of its message to the world. Viewed in this light, the content of the Gospels is taken to be theological rather than historical. Unfortunately, this has caused some scholars to distinguish a supposedly invented "Christ of faith" from the real "Jesus of history." Provided this erroneous distinction is not made, it is important to appreciate that the Gospels are more than biographies. By proclaiming Jesus as the Christ, the four Gospels are designed to transform radically the beliefs and behavior of their readers.

Distinctive Theologies

During the mid-twentieth century, scholars became especially interested in the distinctive features of the Synoptic Gospels. On the one hand, this has helped us understand better the unique contribution of each of the Gospel writers. On the other hand, this has sometimes been taken to an extreme, with too much weight being given to the differences and not enough to the similarities.

Stories

In recent years there has been a growing interest in the Gospels as stories. The reader is not expected to ask historical questions but is rather to be interested in the literary or rhetorical techniques used in telling the story. The strength of this has been to help us appreciate the skill of each author; the weakness has been the lack of interest in historical issues.

CONCLUSION

While all of these approaches contain something of value, they need to be held together in balance if we are to have a proper understanding of the Gospels. The Gospel writers were interested in both the "story" of Jesus and its "significance." Furthermore, the "story" claims to be based on "history." Story, history, and significance are all intertwined. For the Christian reader of the Gospels, it is the significance of what actually happened that creates the "good news" story.

DISCUSSION QUESTIONS

1. The healing of a paralyzed man by Jesus is reported in Matthew 9:1–8, Mark 2:1–12, and Luke 5:17–26. What is noteworthy about how the three Gospels record the incident? How would you explain the similarities and differences?

2. There are two major solutions to the Synoptic Problem. What are these? Why do the majority of New Testament scholars believe that Mark was the first of the Gospels to be composed?

3. Read Luke 1:1–4. What clues may be drawn from this about how Luke set about writing his Gospel? From where might he have gathered information about the life of Jesus?

4. Why is it vital for the Christian faith that the events described in the Gospels took place? What would be lost if we treated them merely as fictional stories?

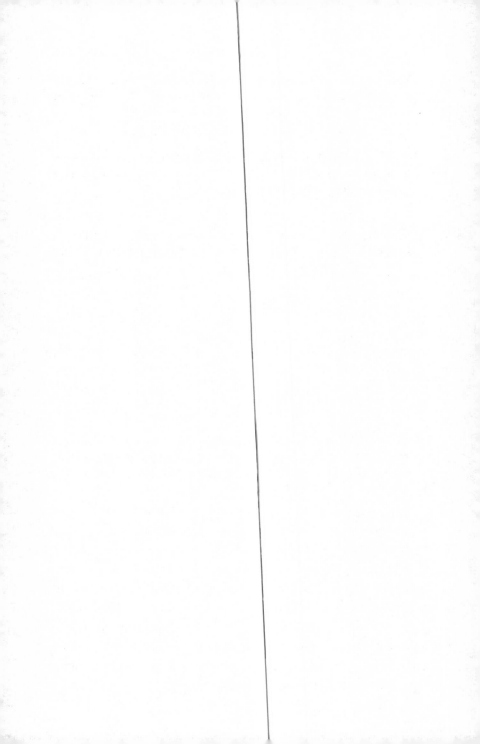

CHAPTER TWELVE

REVIEW AND FINAL OBSERVATIONS

IN THE PRECEDING CHAPTERS we have explored how the four Gospels present complementary pictures of Jesus Christ. From the late first century AD, these four accounts of the life of Jesus were widely read in the early church. Taken together, they provided an authoritative description of Jesus Christ. By portraying him from four different perspectives, the Gospels provide us with a rich picture of this most amazing and unique person. However, the Gospels do not claim to record everything that could be said about Jesus. As the apostle John observes:

> Now there are also many other things that Jesus did. Were every one of them to be written, I suppose that the world itself could not contain the books that would be written. (21:25)

Accepting that there is much more that could have been written about Jesus, the four Gospels nevertheless provide us with sufficient information to grasp the essence of Jesus' nature and mission or vocation. While each Gospel has its own particular emphasis, they are in complete harmony. The fact that all four were read by the earliest Christian communities indicates that they were not viewed as being in competition with one another. They did not present rival views of Jesus Christ. On the contrary, taken together they were perceived as giving a fuller and deeper understanding of Jesus.

To bring this study to a conclusion, and partially by way of review, let us recall briefly the particular themes highlighted by each of the Gospel writers. We began by noting how Mark portrays Jesus as *the Son of God who suffers to ransom others*. In his dynamic portrait of Jesus' adult life, Mark reveals Jesus' unique status as the Son of God. Initially, Jesus' divine nature is displayed through both his remarkable power and the hostility of Satan and his allies. Later, perhaps unexpectedly, Mark reveals that the Son of God's triumph over the powers of evil will be achieved through suffering and death. Reversing normal expectations, Jesus, the Son of God, gives up his life that people may be freed from bondage to Satan and their own sinful human nature. For Mark, the cross is central to Jesus' mission.

Apart from inflicting the cruelest of deaths, crucifixion is an exceptionally humiliating form of execution. There is no glamour or dignity in being nailed to a cross. In making Christ's crucifixion the climax of his Gospel, Mark not only underlines the centrality of the cross for understanding what Jesus achieves, but significantly the cross also defines the nature of Christian discipleship. As Jesus' teaching in Mark 8–10 reveals, his followers are expected to take up the cross daily. Like Jesus, they are to walk the path of humility and give their lives in serving others. The Christian life involves putting other people first rather than asserting our own importance.

Mark's emphasis upon the cross is carried over by Matthew, who repeats almost all that Mark narrates. However, possibly motivated by a desire to persuade Jews of Jesus' importance, Matthew shifts the emphasis in his Gospel to the theme of Jesus as *the son of David who establishes the kingdom of heaven*. Conscious of the long-established tradition that placed the royal house of David at the heart of God's plans for the redemption of humanity, Matthew reworks the contents of Mark's Gospel and introduces additional material that emphasizes Jesus' royal status. From his opening genealogy to Jesus' last words to his disciples, Matthew underlines the reality and significance of Jesus' authority. Throughout the Gospel this authority is demonstrated in Jesus' actions and words, with particular attention being given to his teaching on the kingdom of heaven.

An important aspect of all that Jesus has to say about the kingdom of heaven is its future consummation. Although Jesus' death and resurrection mark the inauguration of the kingdom, he has not come at this stage to judge and punish the wicked. For the present, good and evil people continue to live side-by-side. The good news, however, is an invitation for everyone to embrace Jesus as King. This choice involves adopting a radically different lifestyle governed by attitudes and values that reflect the perfection of God's own holy nature. While membership in the kingdom of heaven is demanding, citizenship is worth everything, as Matthew reminds us through Jesus' parables about treasure in a field and a valuable pearl (Matt. 13:44–46). Some will unfortunately discover that their claim to membership is invalid, for only those who truly submit to Jesus' authority and obey him will be acknowledged by him on his return in regal glory and splendor.

As we have noted, with its emphasis on Jesus as the son of David, Matthew's Gospel appears to be slanted toward Jewish readers. By way of contrast, Luke's Gospel is directed toward a non-Jewish readership. This goes some way toward explaining why Luke presents Jesus as *the Savior of the world who seeks the lost.*

In highlighting this aspect of Jesus' nature, Luke is clearly impressed by the compassion that Jesus shows for those who have been rejected by others. Although Zacchaeus was despised and shunned by his neighbors, Jesus sought him out in the knowledge that this lost son of Abraham needed to be rescued.

Jesus' short visit with him achieved remarkable results. As the story of Zacchaeus reveals, an encounter with Jesus can be a life-transforming experience.

In a society where clear distinctions were drawn between those who were religious and those who were not, Jesus' willingness to embrace the irreligious was highly exceptional. Overturning the conventions of his day, Jesus was frequently found going against the tide. His message that God's love extends to the lost was revolutionary. However, as the parable of the prodigal son graphically reveals, the father's joy at the return of his remorseful younger son is not shared by his older brother. While the compassionate mercy of God is truly good news for the lost, not everyone welcomes the unmerited, pardoning grace of God.

Although the Gospels of Matthew, Mark, and Luke share much in common, John's Gospel is quite distinctive. As we observed, with its emphasis upon the signs that Jesus performed and his pilgrimages to Jerusalem for various feasts, John's account has a very different feel to it. To appreciate why John presents the good news in this fashion, we need to grasp that he wishes to affirm that Jesus is *the Lamb of God who brings eternal life through a new exodus.*

John's presentation of Jesus is influenced by his understanding of the divine rescue of the Israelites from Egypt recorded in the book of Exodus. John views Jesus as achieving an even greater deliverance. As the blood of the Passover sacrifice saved the firstborn male Israelites from death, so John sees the sacrifice of Jesus as life giving. Remarkably, it is eternal life that Jesus gives to those who believe in him.

As an aid to remembering the distinctive thrust of each Gospel, their portraits of Jesus may be summarized as follows:

• In Mark, Jesus is the Son of God who suffers to ransom others.

- In Matthew, Jesus is the son of David who establishes the kingdom of heaven.
- In Luke, Jesus is the Savior of the world who seeks the lost.
- In John, Jesus is the Lamb of God who brings eternal life through a new exodus.

While these summaries serve a useful purpose in reminding us of the special emphasis of each Gospel, we need to be careful that we do not reduce Jesus to a few factual statements. It is very easy to say, "Jesus is Lord and Savior." But do we always grasp the full significance and weight of these words? In a very important way the Gospel accounts prevent Jesus from becoming a mere fact. As we read them we encounter a real person, someone with whom we can identify, even though he is so utterly different from us.

And as we read the Gospels with an open mind, we soon discover that we cannot account for Jesus Christ in terms of his being an ordinary, or even extraordinary, human being. His exceptional nature requires that we take seriously the claim that he is divine. C. S. Lewis draws out the significance of this:

> A man who was merely a man and said the sort of things Jesus said would not be a great moral teacher. He would either be a lunatic—on a level with the man who says he is a poached egg—or else he would be the Devil of Hell. You must make your choice. Either this man was, and is, the Son of God: or else a madman or something worse. You can shut Him up for a fool, you can spit at Him and kill Him as a demon; or you can fall at His feet and call Him Lord and God. But let us not come with any patronizing nonsense about His being a great human teacher. He has not left that open to us. He did not intend to.[1]

As Lewis perceptively acknowledges, Jesus cannot be easily categorized as merely a man. There is too much about him that

---

[1]C. S. Lewis, *Mere Christianity* (London: Fontanta, 1955), 52–53.

defies purely human explanations. Beginning with Mark, all of the Gospels affirm unambiguously Jesus' divine nature.

Nor is the proclamation of Jesus' divine nature limited to the Gospels. Paul's letter to the Christians in Colossae contains one of the greatest summary statements regarding the person of Jesus Christ. Writing about AD 60, Paul says of Jesus:

> He is the image of the invisible God, the firstborn of all creation. For by him all things were created, in heaven and on earth, visible and invisible, whether thrones or dominions or rulers or authorities—all things were created through him and for him. And he is before all things, and in him all things hold together. And he is the head of the body, the church. He is the beginning, the firstborn from the dead, that in everything he might be preeminent. For in him all the fullness of God was pleased to dwell, and through him to reconcile to himself all things, whether on earth or in heaven, making peace by the blood of his cross. And you, who once were alienated and hostile in mind, doing evil deeds, he has now reconciled in his body of flesh by his death, in order to present you holy and blameless and above reproach before him, if indeed you continue in the faith, stable and steadfast, not shifting from the hope of the gospel that you heard, which has been proclaimed in all creation under heaven, and of which I, Paul, became a minister. (Col. 1:15–23)

As the concluding words of this passage highlight, this summary reflects "the gospel," the good news that is set out in more detail in Matthew, Mark, Luke, and John. As we focus on Jesus, we continually need to remind ourselves that the Gospels are more than "good news"; they are "great news."

For the Christian, nothing is more vital than being overwhelmed by the wonder of Jesus Christ. If we are to obey his summons to follow him and take up the cross each day, more than anything else, we need to be convinced of his uniqueness and overwhelmed by what he has done for us. Not surprisingly, the depth of our Christian commitment will mirror our love for Jesus. Like the woman who anointed Jesus' feet with oil in Mark 14:1–9, we need to be so moved that we, too, desire to lavish generously on him all that we have, with no hint of embarrassment.

Nothing matches the experience of discovering personally the unmerited, sacrificial love of Jesus for us. Although our supposed knowledge of the Gospels may sometimes discourage us from reading them as we should, hopefully this short study will provide a fresh impetus to reexamine them and discover anew the most unique and incredible "man" who ever lived and continues to live.

DISCUSSION QUESTIONS

1. As a result of looking at the four Gospels, how has your understanding of Jesus deepened? What has made the biggest impression upon you?

2. Each of the four Gospels stresses a different aspect of Jesus, involving his nature and vocation. How do these different presentations complement one another?

3. The first chapter of each Gospel is quite different. How does each opening chapter reflect the distinctive emphasis of that Gospel?

4. Apart from giving four different perspectives on Jesus, are there any other advantages in having four Gospels?

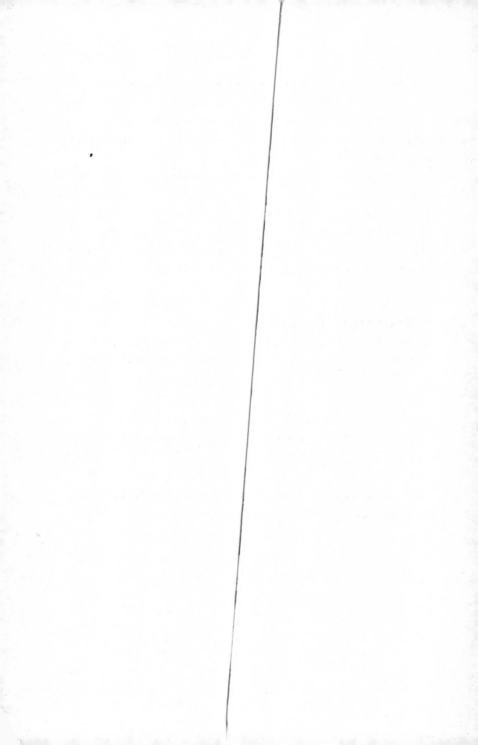

FURTHER READING

HUNDREDS, IF NOT THOUSANDS, of books and articles on the Gospels are published every year. The following are but a small selection, chosen because they provide a balanced discussion of the main issues in modern Gospel scholarship. They are helpful resources for those seeking more detailed information.

GENERAL INTRODUCTIONS TO THE GOSPELS:

Blomberg, Craig L. *Jesus and the Gospels: An Introduction and Survey*. 2nd ed. Nashville, TN: Broadman, 2009.

Carson, D. A., and Douglas J. Moo. *An Introduction to the New Testament*. 2nd ed. Grand Rapids, MI: Zondervan, 2005.

Stanton, G. N. *The Gospels and Jesus*. 2nd ed. New York: Oxford University Press, 2002.

Walton, S., and D. Wenham. *Introducing the Gospels and Acts*, Vol. 1, Exploring the New Testament. London: SPCK, 2001.

FOR A MORE COMPREHENSIVE TREATMENT OF PARTICULAR TOPICS:

Green, Joel B., Scot McKnight, and I. Howard Marshall, eds. *Dictionary of Jesus and the Gospels*. The IVP Bible Dictionary Series. Downers Grove, IL: InterVarsity, 1992.

ON THE HISTORICITY OF THE GOSPELS:

Blomberg, Craig L. *The Historical Reliability of John's Gospel*. 2nd ed. Downers Grove, IL: InterVarsity, 2007.

_____. *The Historical Reliability of the Gospels*. Downers Grove, IL: InterVarsity, 1987.

ONE-VOLUME COMMENTARY ON THE WHOLE BIBLE:

Carson, D. A., R. T. France, J. A. Motyer, and Gordon. J. Wenham, eds. *New Bible Commentary: 21st Century Edition.* Downers Grove, IL: InterVarsity, 1994.

COMMENTARIES ON INDIVIDUAL GOSPELS:

Matthew

Blomberg, Craig L. *Matthew.* Vol. 22, The New American Commentary. Nashville, TN: Broadman, 1992.*

Carson, D. A. *Matthew.* Vol. 1, Expositor's Bible Commentary, ed. F. E. Gaebelein. Grand Rapids, MI: Zondervan, 1984.

France, R. T. *The Gospel According to Matthew: An Introduction and Commentary.* Tyndale New Testament Commentaries. Grand Rapids, MI: Eerdmans, 1985.*

Morris, Leon. *The Gospel According to Matthew.* The Pillar New Testament Commentary. Grand Rapids, MI: Eerdmans, 1992.

Mark

Cole, R. Alan. *The Gospel According to Mark: An Introduction and Commentary.* Tyndale New Testament Commentaries. Grand Rapids, MI: Eerdmans, 1989.*

Edwards, James. *The Gospel According to Mark.* The Pillar New Testament Commentary. Grand Rapids, MI: Eerdmans, 2002.

Hurtado, Larry W. *Mark.* New International Biblical Commentary. Peabody, MA: Hendrickson, 1995.*

Luke

Bock, Darrell L. *Luke.* IVP New Testament Commentaries. Nottingham, UK: Inter-Varsity, 1995.*

Stein, Robert H. *Luke.* Vol. 22, The New American Commentary. Nashville, TN: Broadman, 2003.

John

Carson, D. A. *The Gospel According to John.* The Pillar New Testament Commentary. Leicester, UK: Apollos, 1991.

Kruse, Colin G. *John.* Tyndale New Testament Commentaries. Grand Rapids, MI: Eerdmans, 2004.*

(* more suitable for beginners)

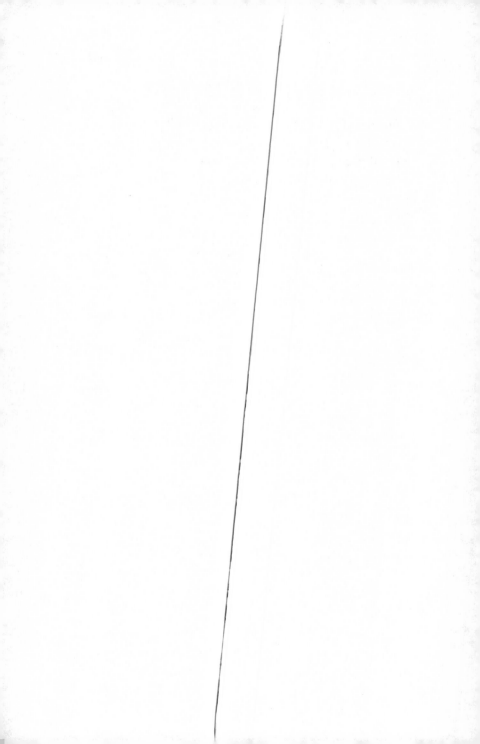

GENERAL INDEX

ascension, 24

baptism, 82–83, 99
Barnabas, 40
Beatitudes, 119
belief, 102–3, 108

church expansion, 22, 37, 81, 85, 94
crucifixion, 34–35, 55–57, 91, 101, 128

discipleship, 51–58, 128

eternal life, 107, 113–14, 130–31
evil, 33–34
exodus, 35, 109–10
See also new exodus
exorcisms, 25

faith, 37–38
feasts, 110–11

Galilee, 19–20, 100
genealogy, 60, 69–70, 90
Gentiles, 35–37, 42, 77, 94–95
God

kingdom of, 31–33
love of, 130
presence of, 65
Good Samaritan, 24
Gospels
composition of, 117–24
definition of, 17–18
geographic sequence of, 118–19
historicity of, 123–24
See also Synoptic Gospels
grace, 130
Griesbach, Johann, 118, 121–22

healings, 54, 70
heaven, kingdom of, 31, 60, 73–74, 76–78, 128–29
Holy Spirit, 81–85
humility, 57
hymns, 95

Ignatius, 59
Irenaeus, 97–98

Jerusalem, 19–20, 24–25, 100
Jesus
authority of, 33, 65